# Dasy Ravid – Painter

Published by: Yotzrim Art Gallery - Consulting and selling art
Design: Roni oz

© All rights reserved to Yotzrim Art Gallery - Consulting and Sale of Art- 2021
www.yotzrimgallery.com

Address: PO Box 5123, Herzliya, ZIP Code 4649719
Phone: +972-54-5286808

Do not reproduce, copy, photograph, record, translate, store in a database, transmit or receive in any way or transmit data from it in any form or electronic means, optical or mechanical or otherwise - any part of the material in this book. Commercial use of any kind of material contained in this book is strictly prohibited without the prior permission of the creators of the gallery.

# *Dasy Ravid*
## Painter

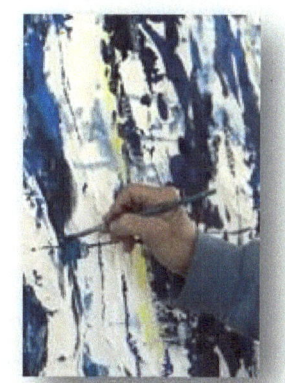

Member of Kibbutz Gvaram.
Born in Tel Aviv **1955**
Member of Association of Artists and Sculptors, Ashkelon.

*Art, for me, is the language of lines, marks, form and colour.*
*This is a language that has no mistakes, no right and no wrong.*
*In this way I present what I absorb, feel, understand and express.*
*This is a way to represent myself.*

**Professional background**:
Studied art at Oranim Art Seminar, and Art Therapy at Seminar HaKibbutzim.
Studied under the artists: Arie Rothman, Ilana Sela, Pnina Ben Gal, Benny Shemesh and Eli Tsarfati.
Worked as art therapist for 20 years at Barzilai Hospital, Children's Psychiatric Department.
Art therapist with traumatized patients, Community Reinforcement Centre, Ashkelon Area Regional Council.
Many years' experience supporting adults and children with special needs.

# Dasy Ravid
## Painter

**Awards:**

Award from Judge A. Loizara and A. Alkalai, representative of the Association of Artists and Sculptors.

Participated in ZOA exhibition where awarded prize by Mrs. Geula Rabinowitz, wife of mayor of Tel Aviv – Jaffa.

Participation in Exhibitions:

Helena Rubinstein Pavillion for Contemporary Art, Tel Aviv Museum, group exhibition curated by Telila Bisht.

Ministry of Education, group exhibition.

Cultural Hall of Kibbutz Nir Yisrael, group exhibition.

Kibbutz Gvaram, solo exhibition where many works were bought.

Art Association of Ashkelon, group exhibition.

Internet gallery of creation, original Israeli art, group exhibition.

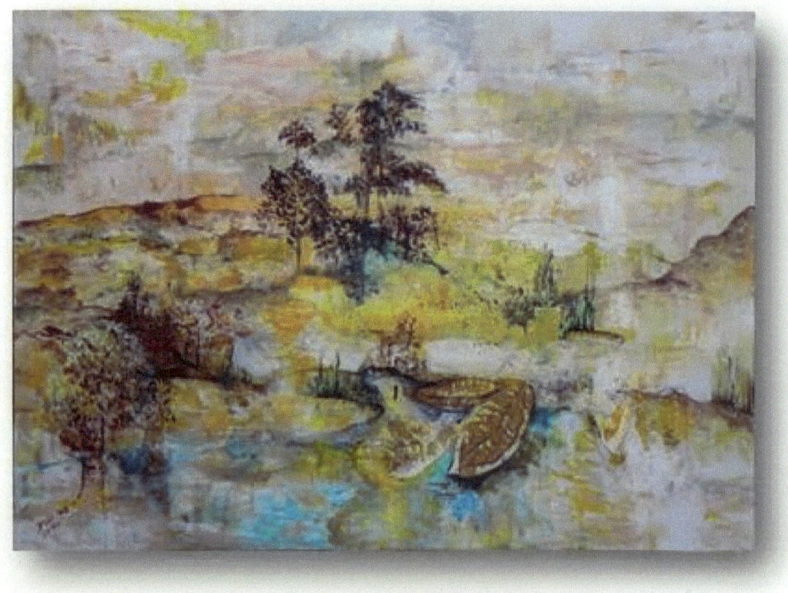

## How I work

Today I work in my home, from within my personal and therapeutic world. I make a line, mark or form. I look at them from different angles, and between the lines, I create for myself a story born from line, mark and colour.

The drawings are not planned in advance. They are created out of the material.

They surprise me and bring me happiness and a smile of new creation.

The grey form is created from observing marks, colour and lines that are shown and drawn between actual dried cactus.

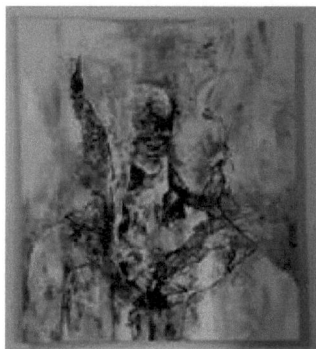

We (our family) frequently wander the country by foot. On one of our treks, in Nahal Shefer, in the Galil, we gathered dried plants and leaves, as is our custom. I later glued the cactus leaves onto the anvas and spread Gesso (combination of glue+chalk) over it. I emphasized some of the lines.

I looked at the canvas and rotated it. I repeated this a few more times, each time working on the material from a different angle.

And suddenly a form looked out of the canvas, leading me to strengthen it with a few more details and lines.

Suddenly it had a presence. I felt it must remain on the canvas.

The form with the kerchief was created behind the kerchief, in the period of the first Coronavirus lockdown.

Maybe there is something of the unconscious here, connected with the mask.

While working I tend to use sandwich wrapping paper.
I do not have a palette for mixing colours.

Sometimes some surplus colour remains on the paper, and it is a pity to throw it away.

Here, in this painting, I used paint that was left
over on the sandwich paper. I transferred it to the canvas like
a print – I spread the paper with the paint from my previous work
over the canvas and then lifted the paper off.

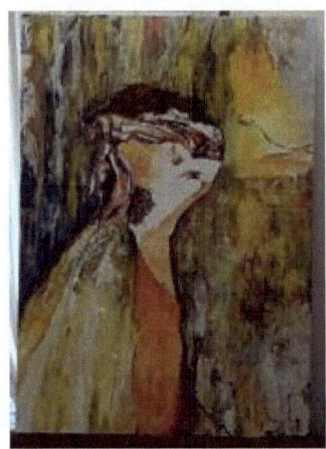

I have returned to this process a number of times.
I looked at the painting from different angles, extended a few lines
and suddenly I saw the kerchief with a knot at the side.

The image was exposed, it grew out of the kerchief with all its power
and strength, it took on presence and colour.

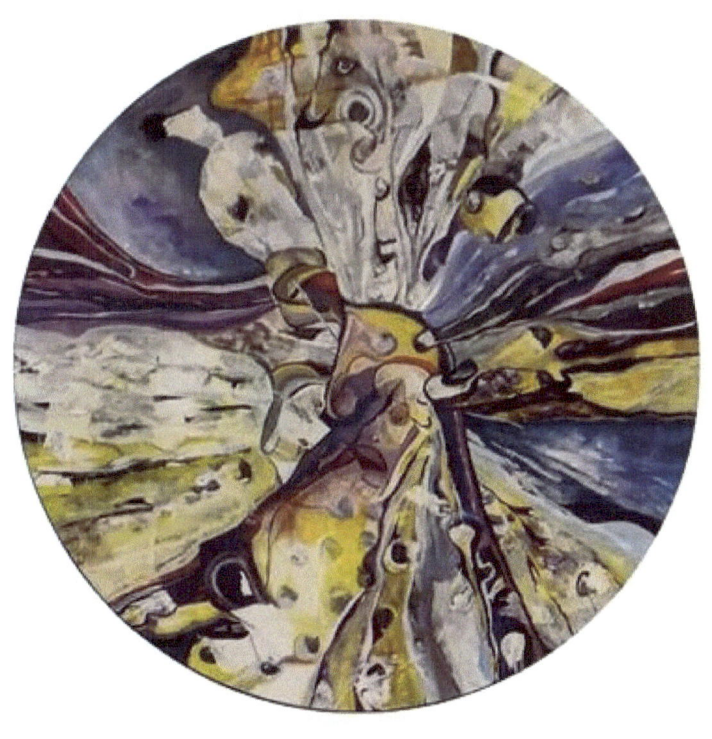

Acrylic on canvas, diameter 96 cm

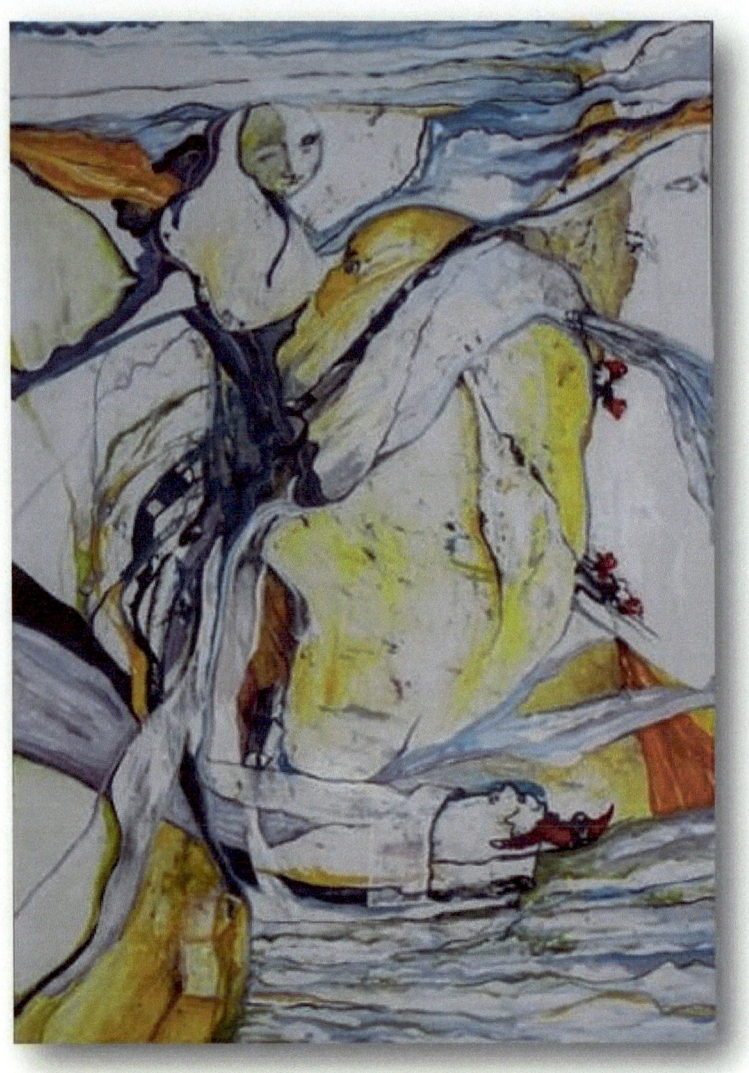

Acrylic on canvas, 99 by 68 cm

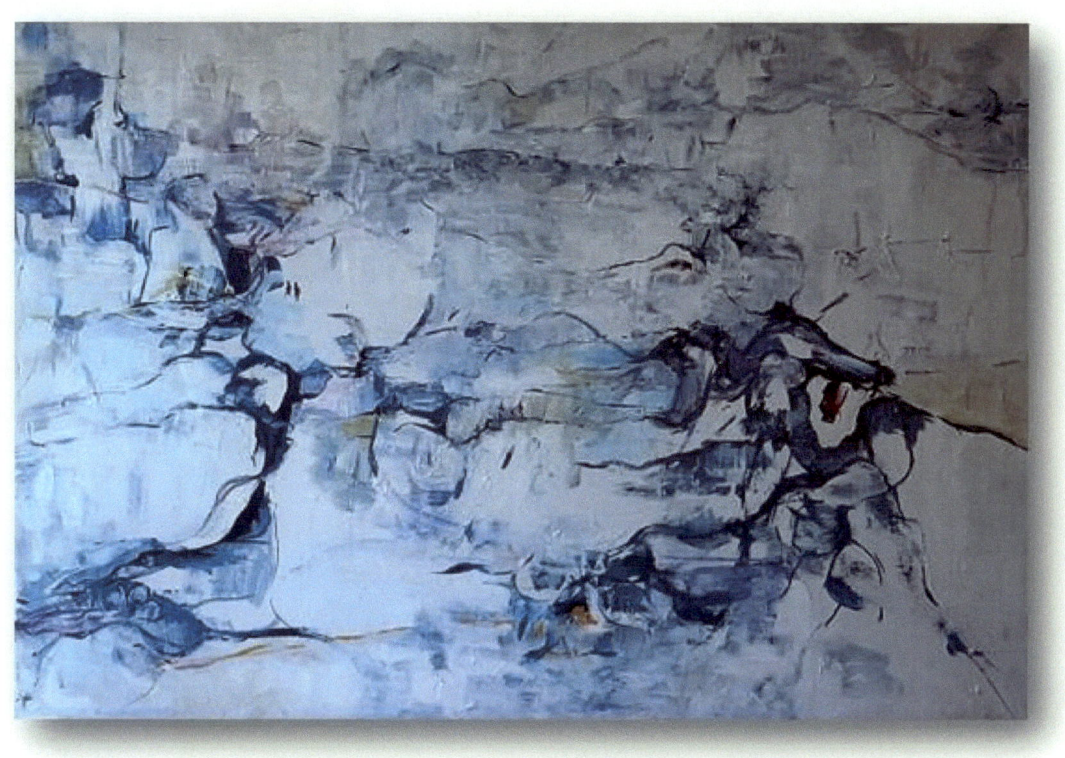

Acrylic on canvas, 68 by 98 cm

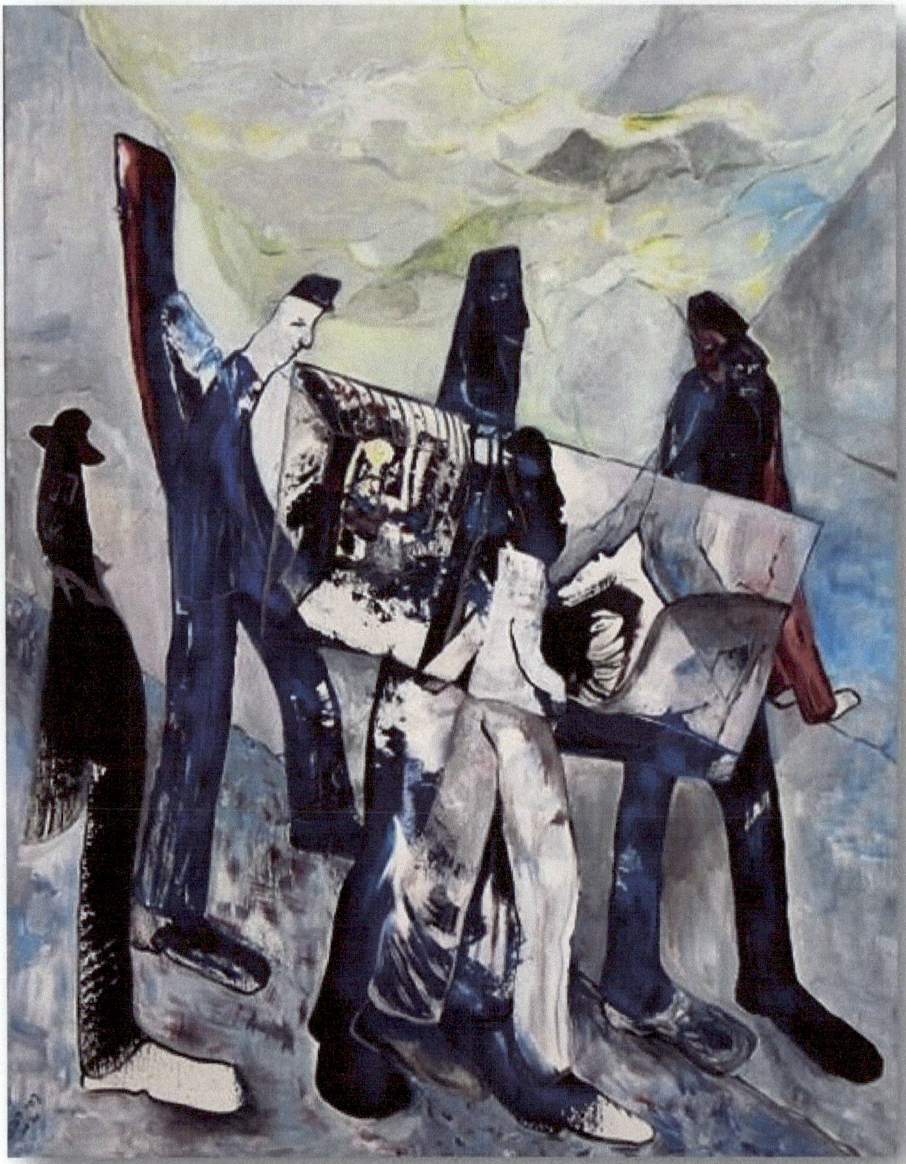

Acrylic on canvas, 80 by 60 cm

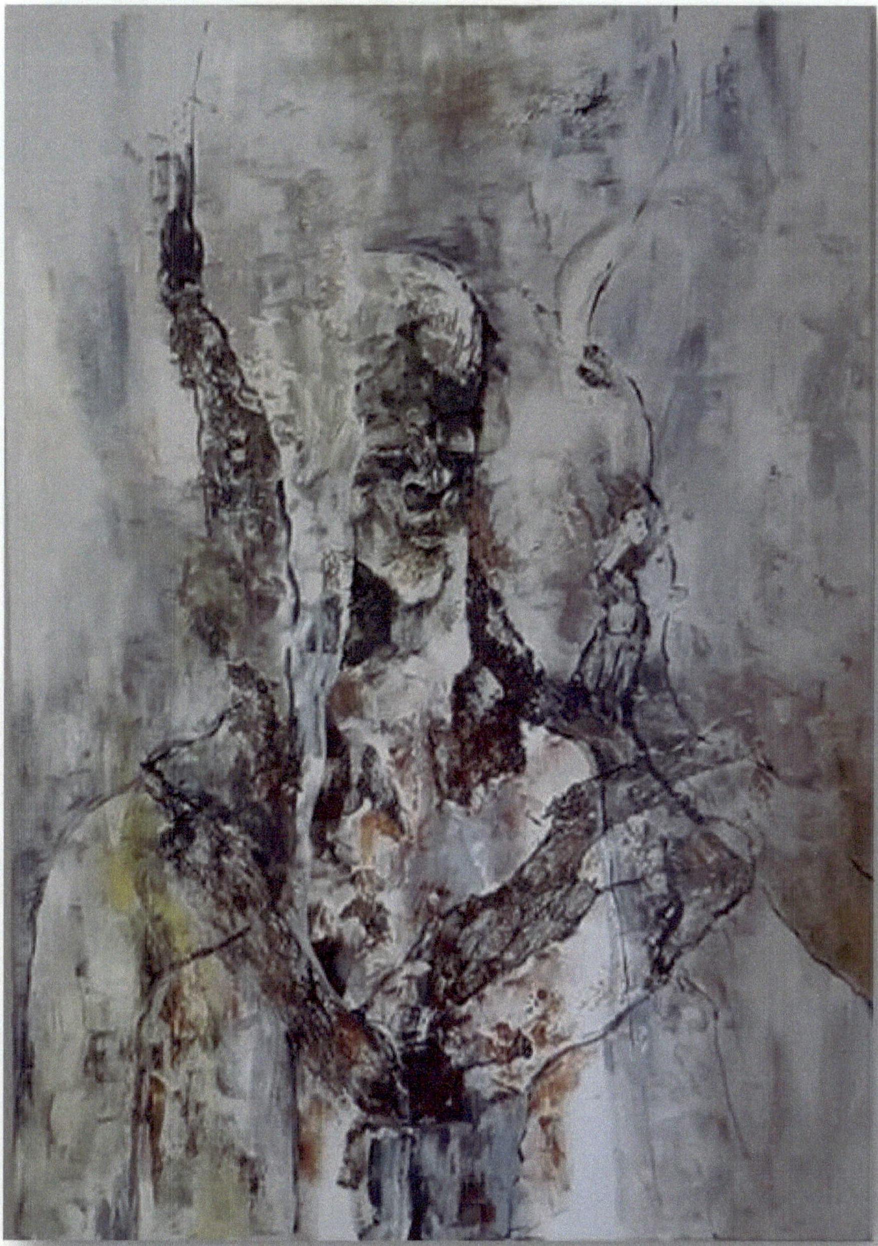

Acrylic on canvas, 100 by 70 cm

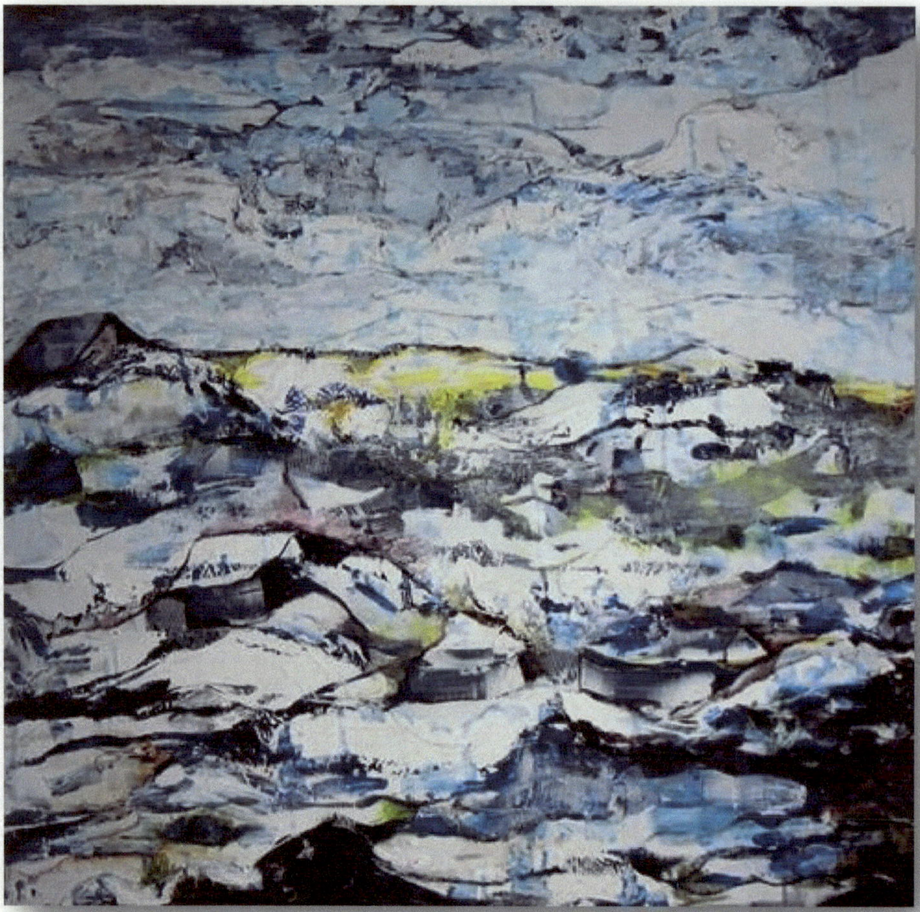

Acrylic on canvas, 90 by 90 cm

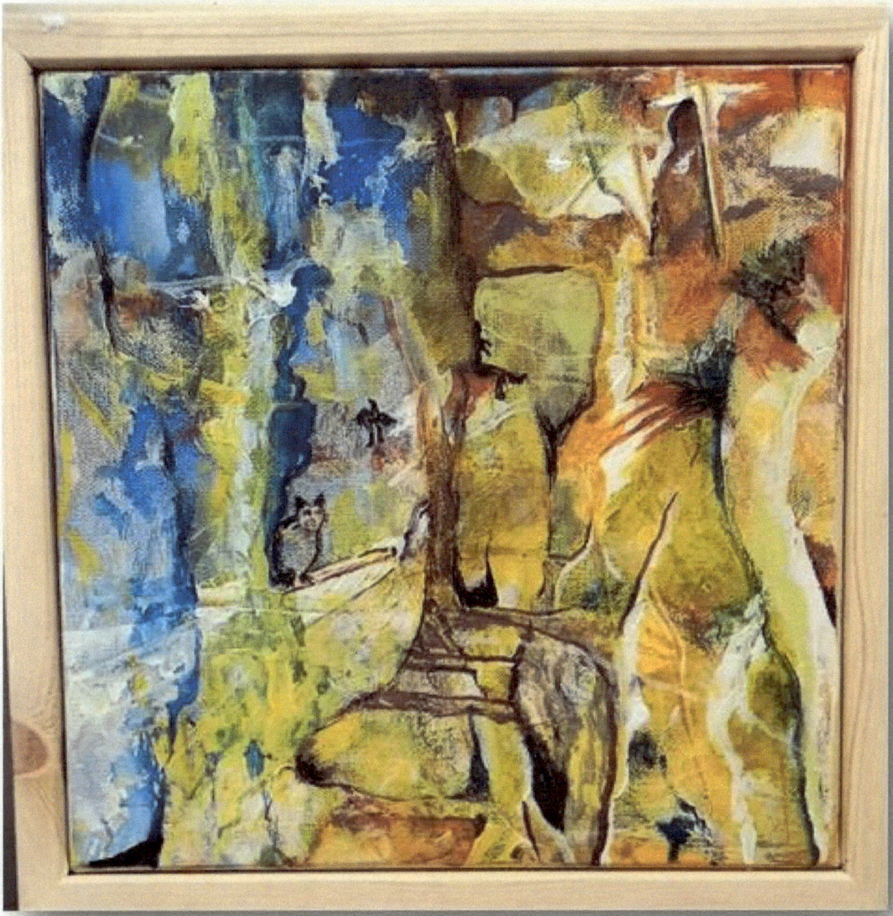

Acrylic on canvas, 28 by 28 cm

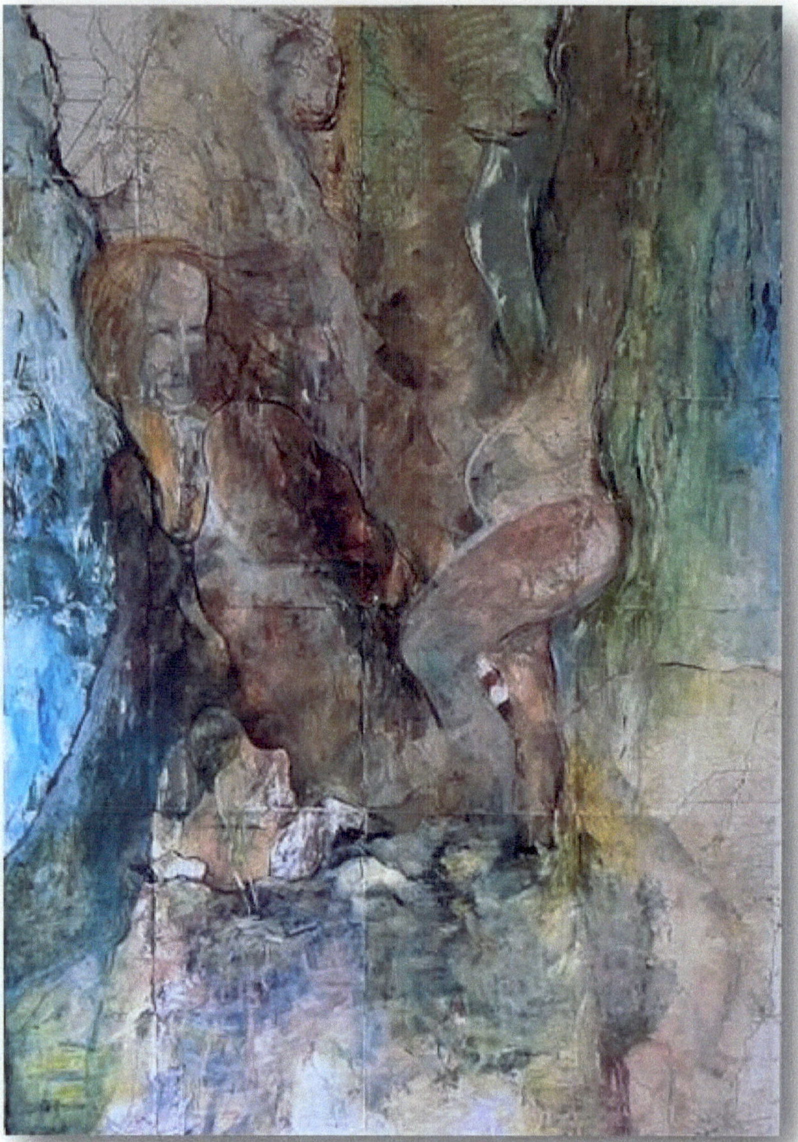

Acrylic on cardboard, 100 by 70 cm

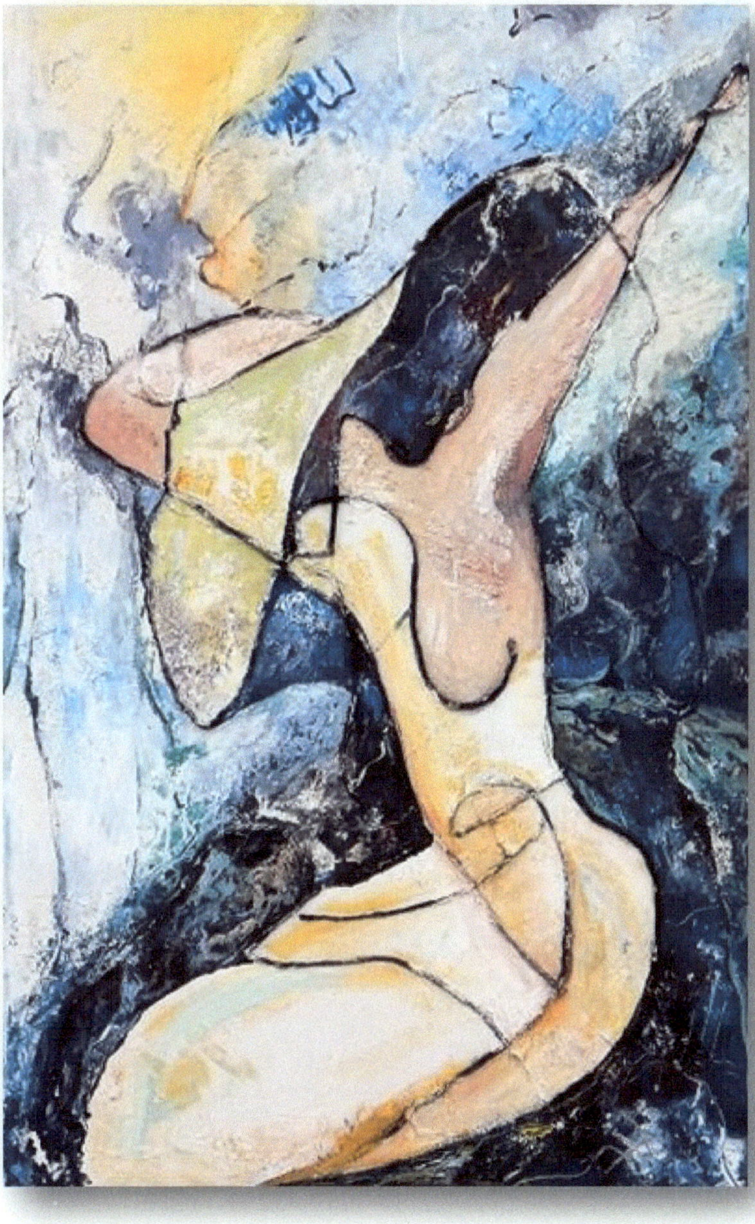

Acrylic on canvas, 100 by 70 cm

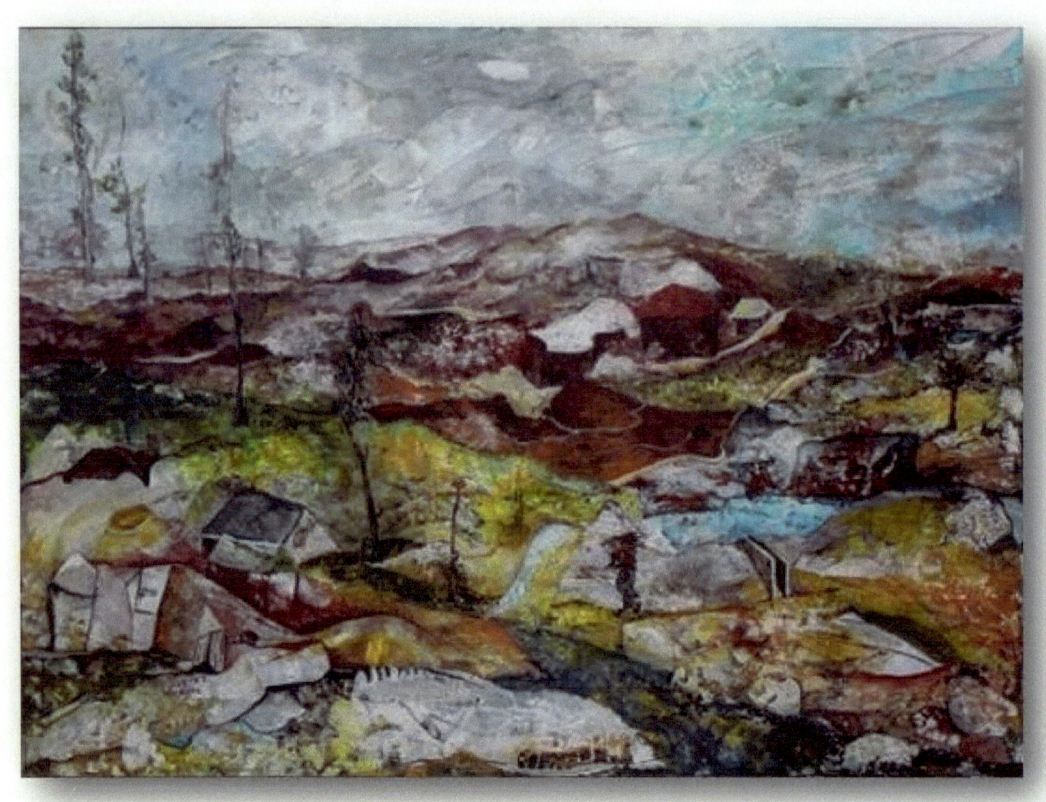

Acrylic on canvas, 94 by 124 cm

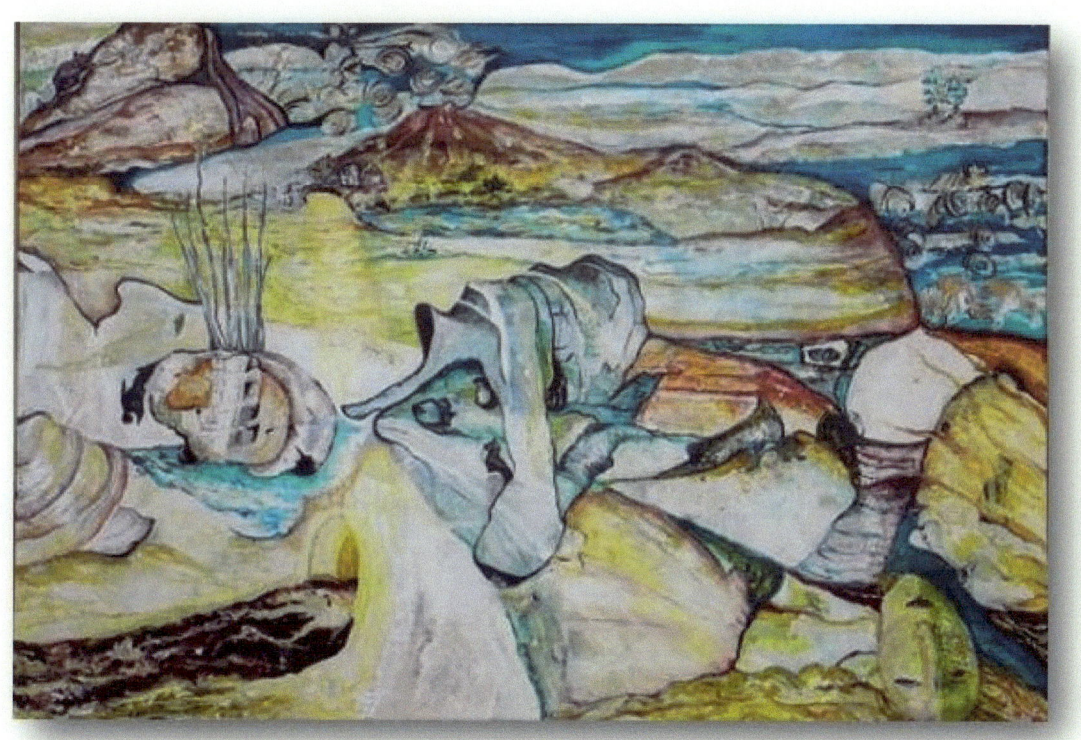

Acrylic on canvas, 70 by 100 cm

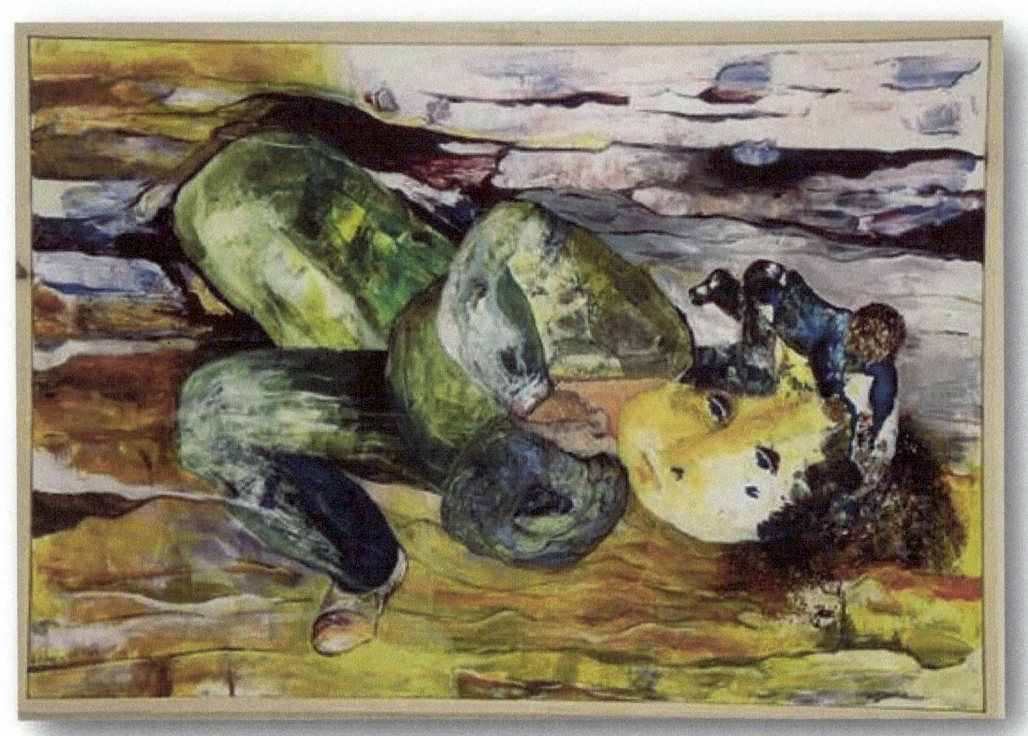

Acrylic on canvas, 70 by 100 cm

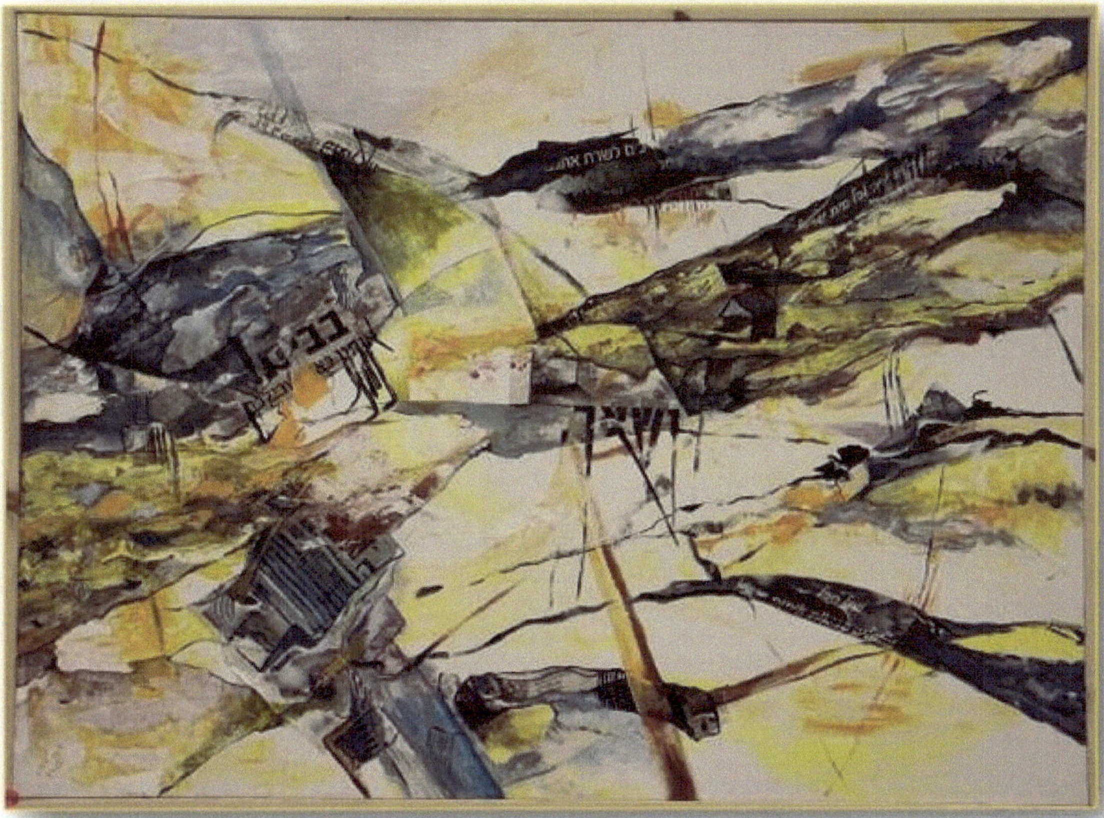

Acrylic on canvas, 100 by 120 cm

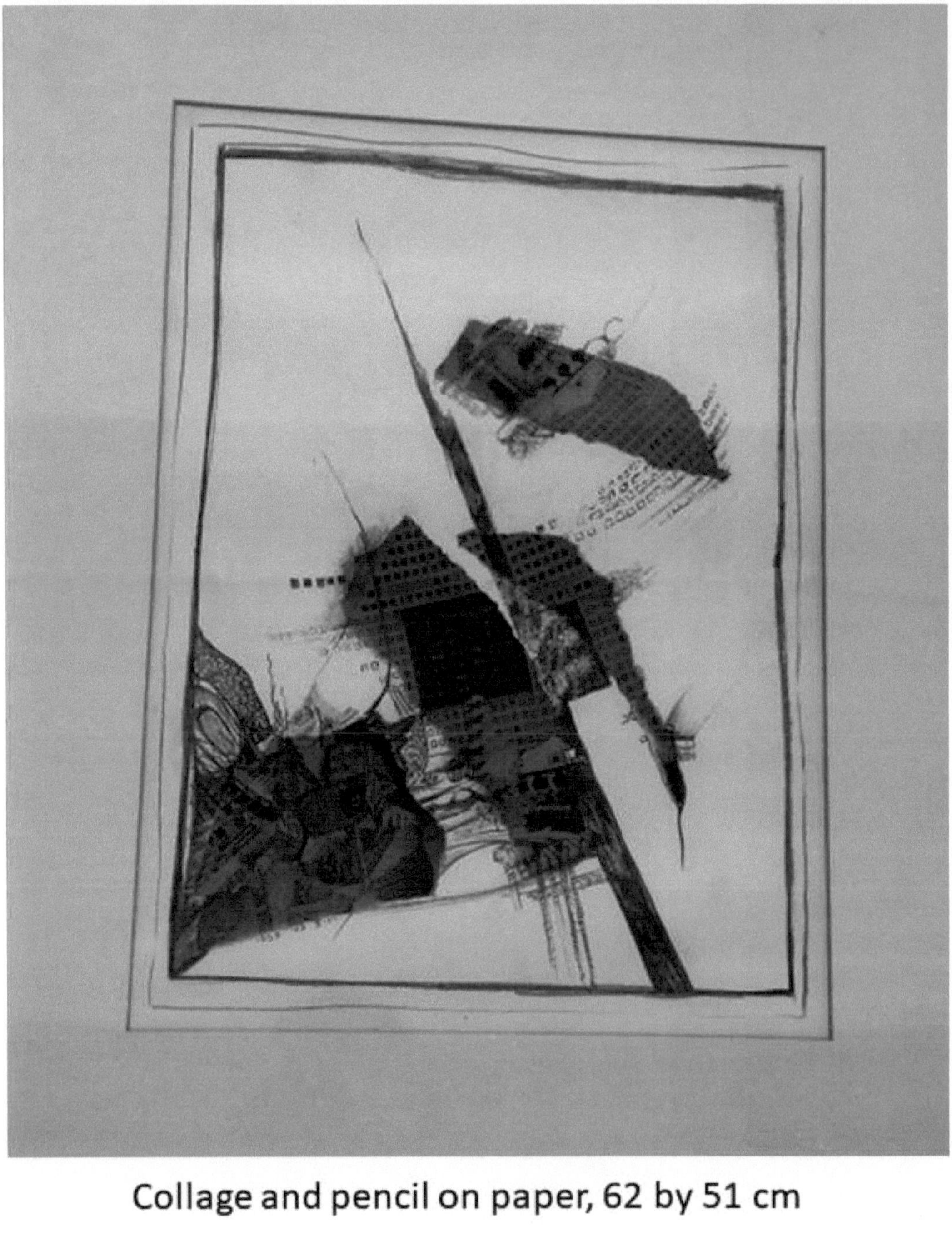

Collage and pencil on paper, 62 by 51 cm

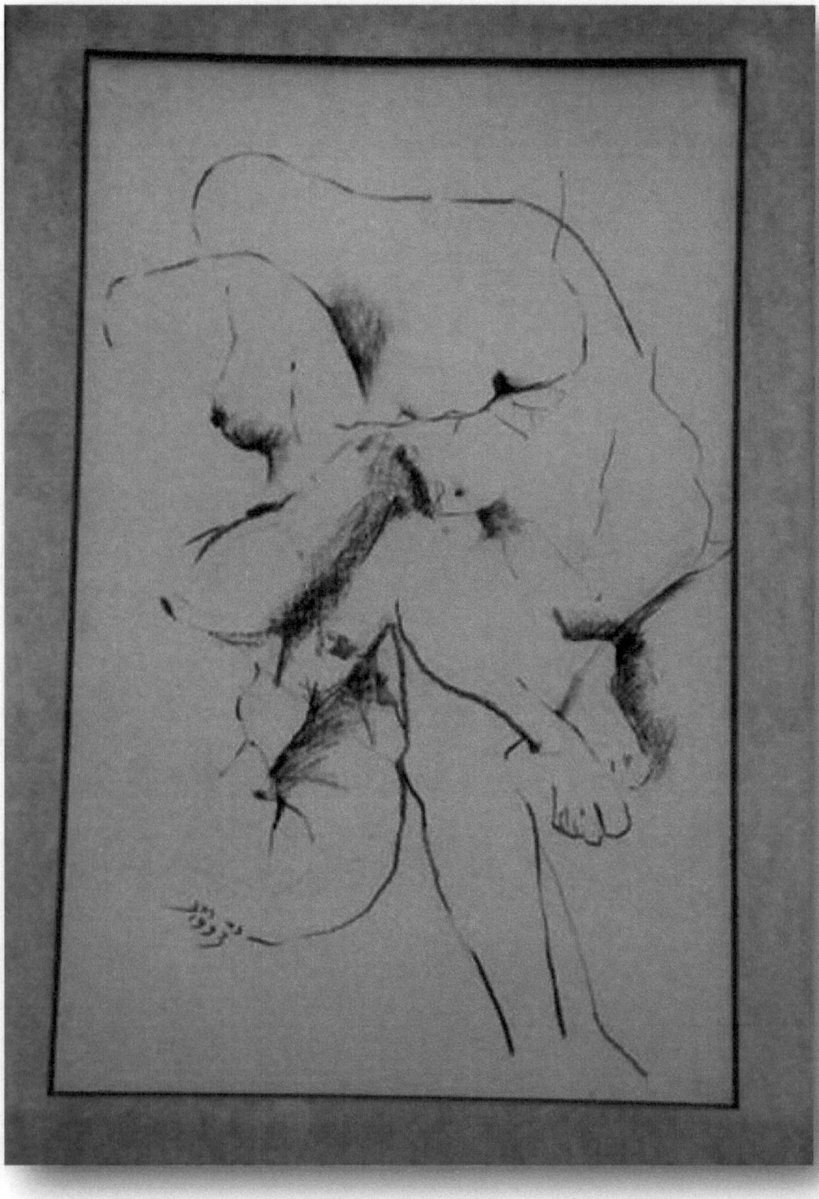

Drawing in pencil on paper, 76 by 54 cm

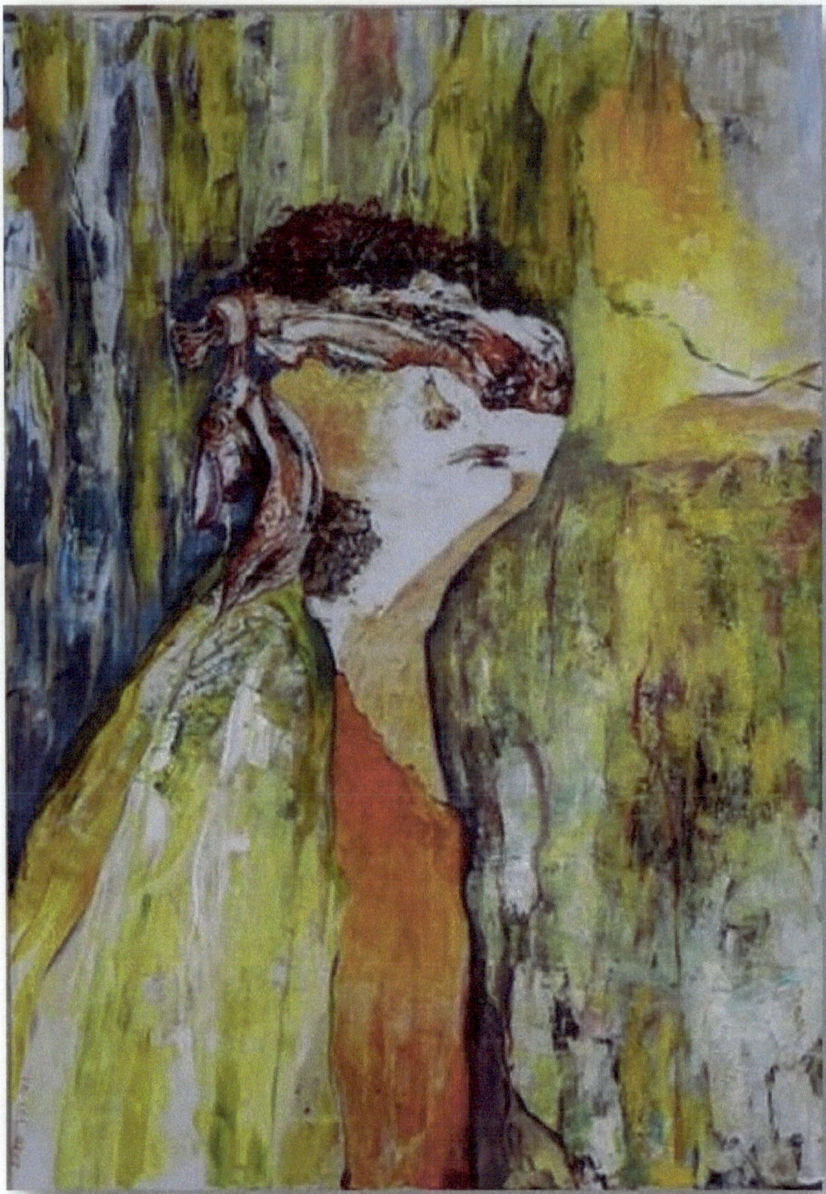

Acrylic on canvas, 100 by 70 cm

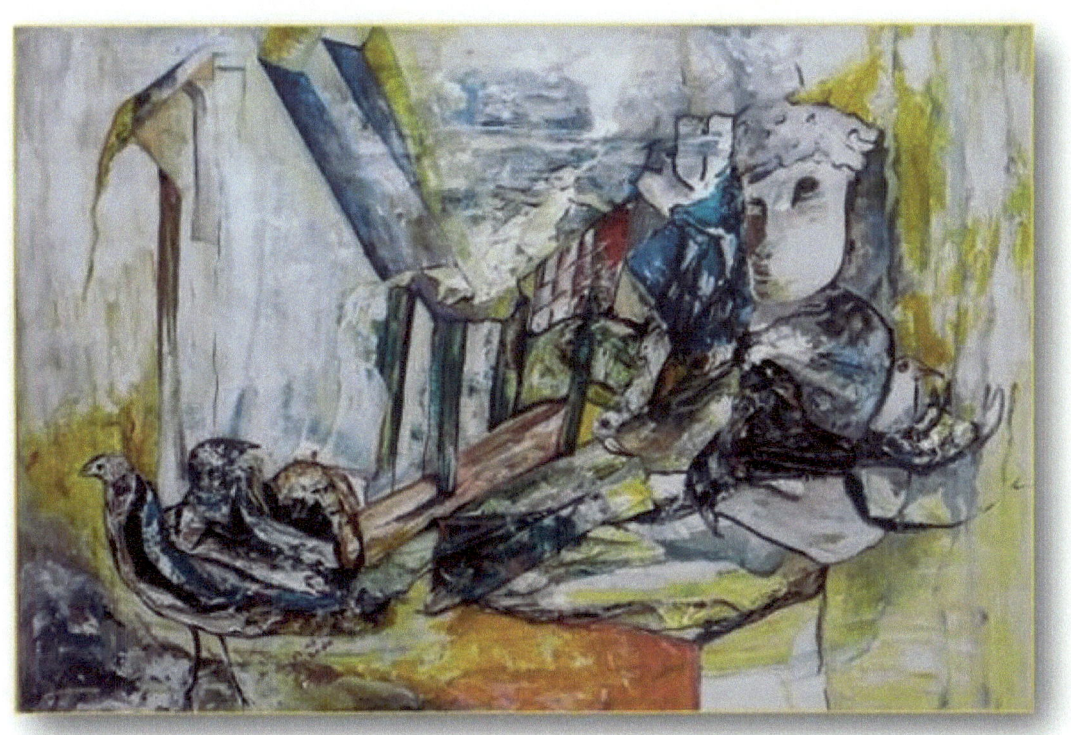

Mix media and acrylic on canvas, 70 by 100 cm

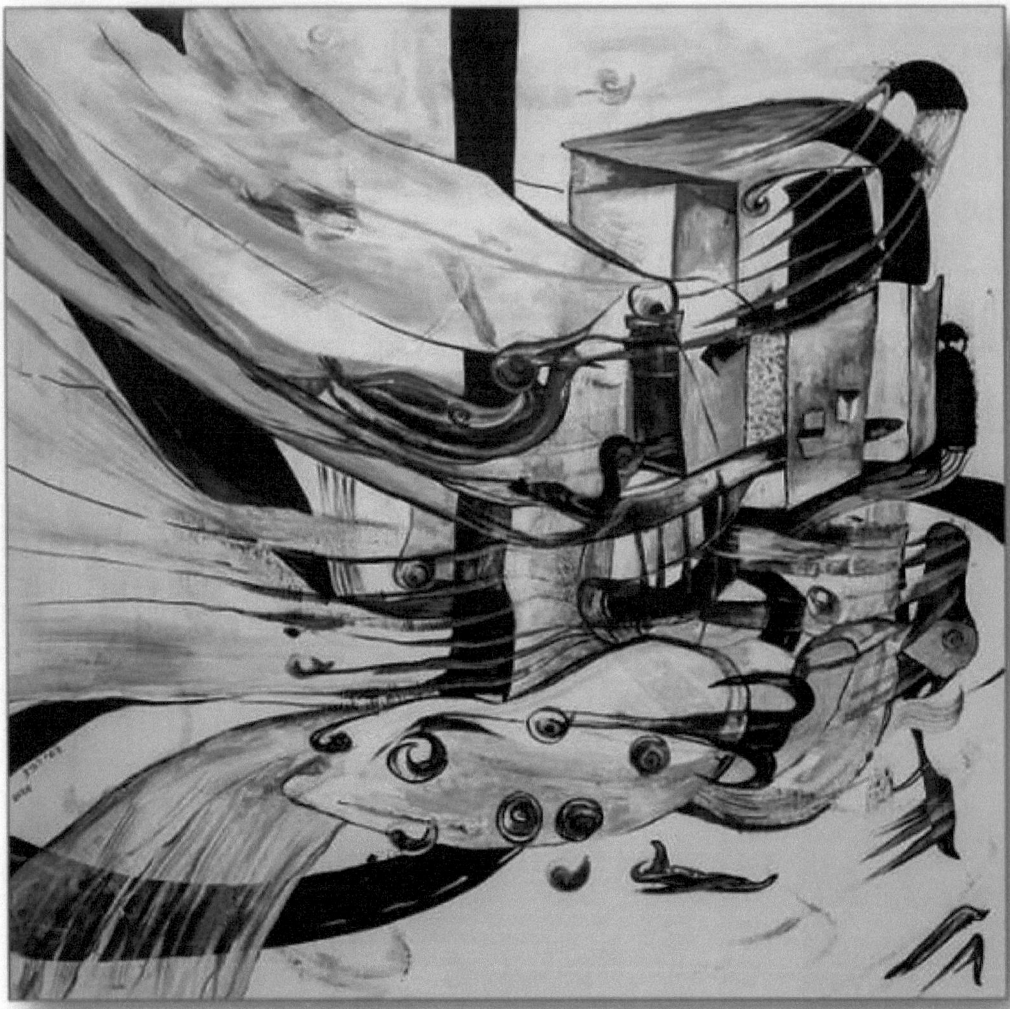

Acrylic on canvas, 90 by 90 cm

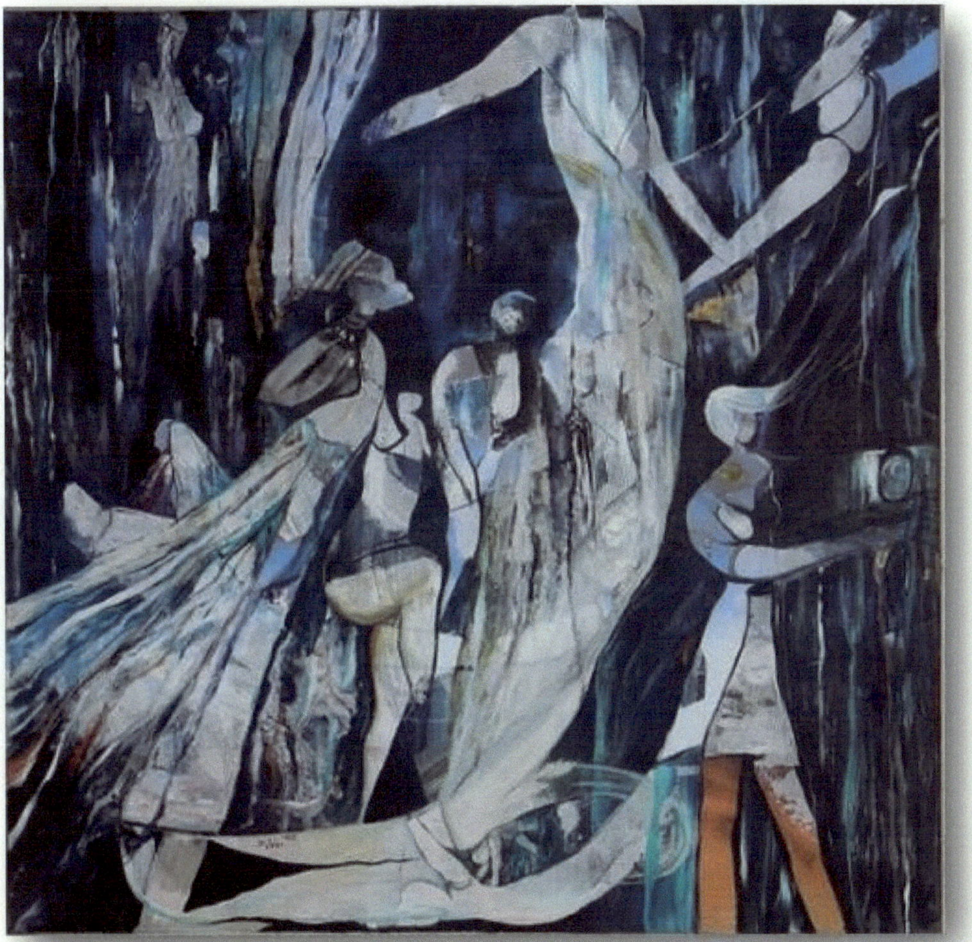

Acrylic on canvas, 110 by 110 cm

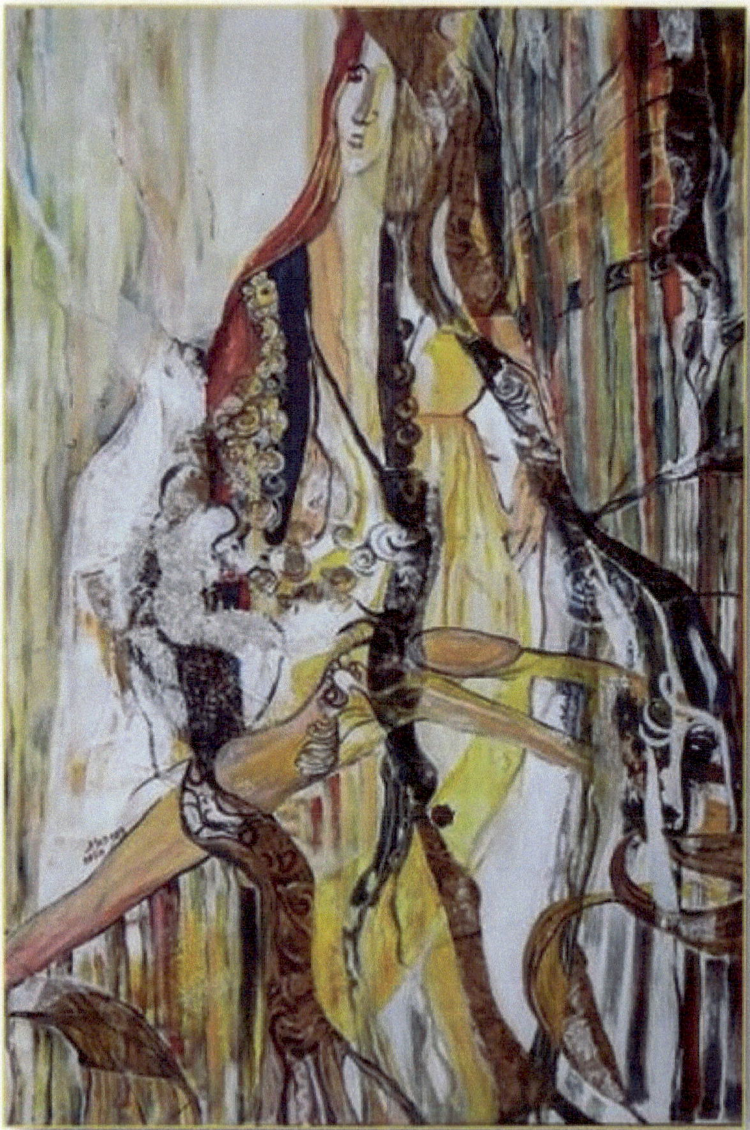

Acrylic on canvas, 123 by 83 cm

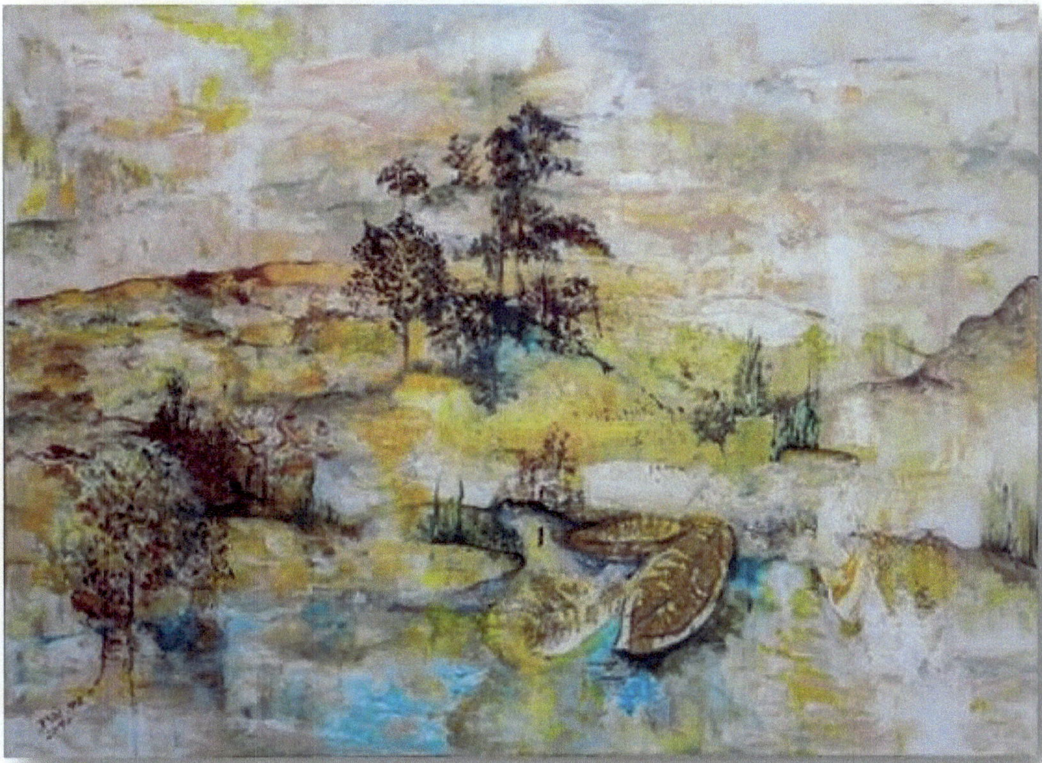

Acrylic on canvas, 60 by 90 cm

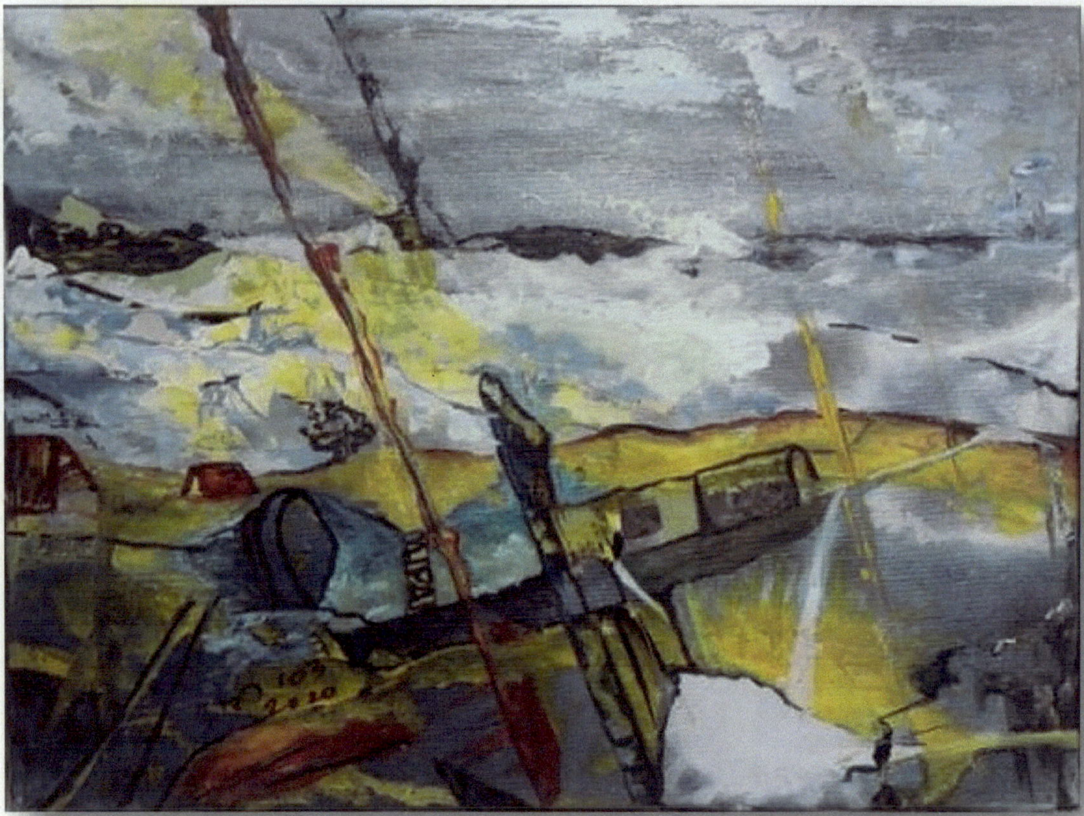

Acrylic on canvas, 30 by 40 cm

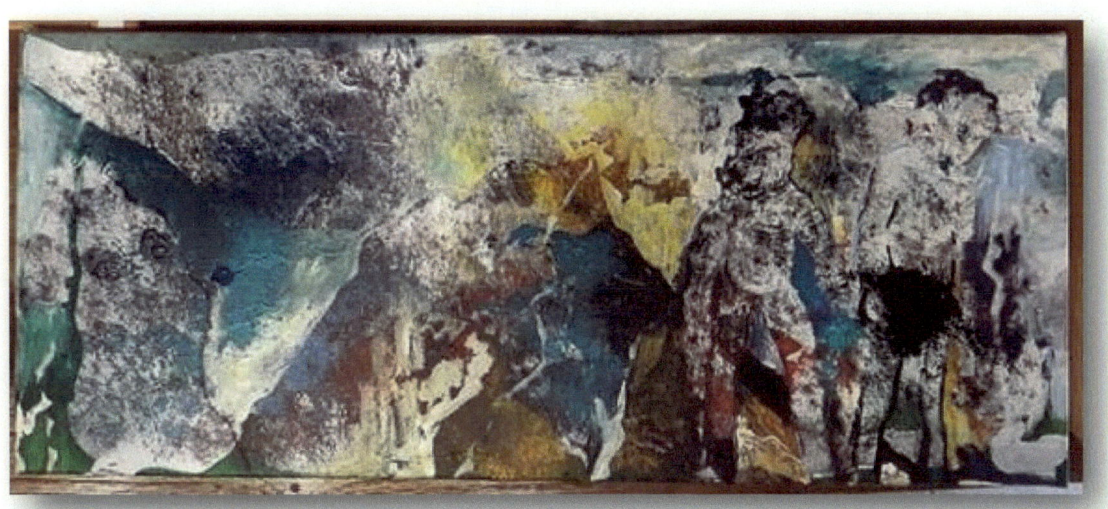

Acrylic on canvas, 30 by 70 cm

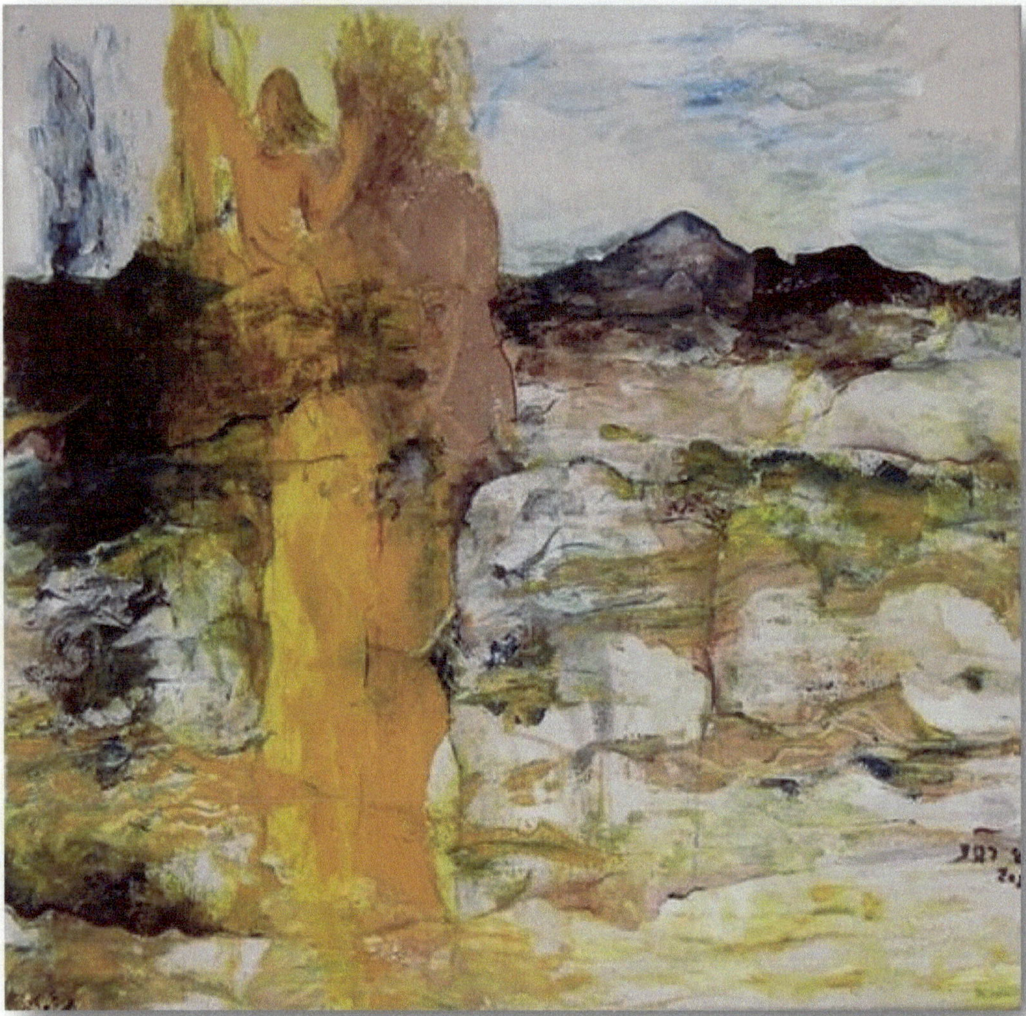

Acrylic on canvas, 50 by 60 cm

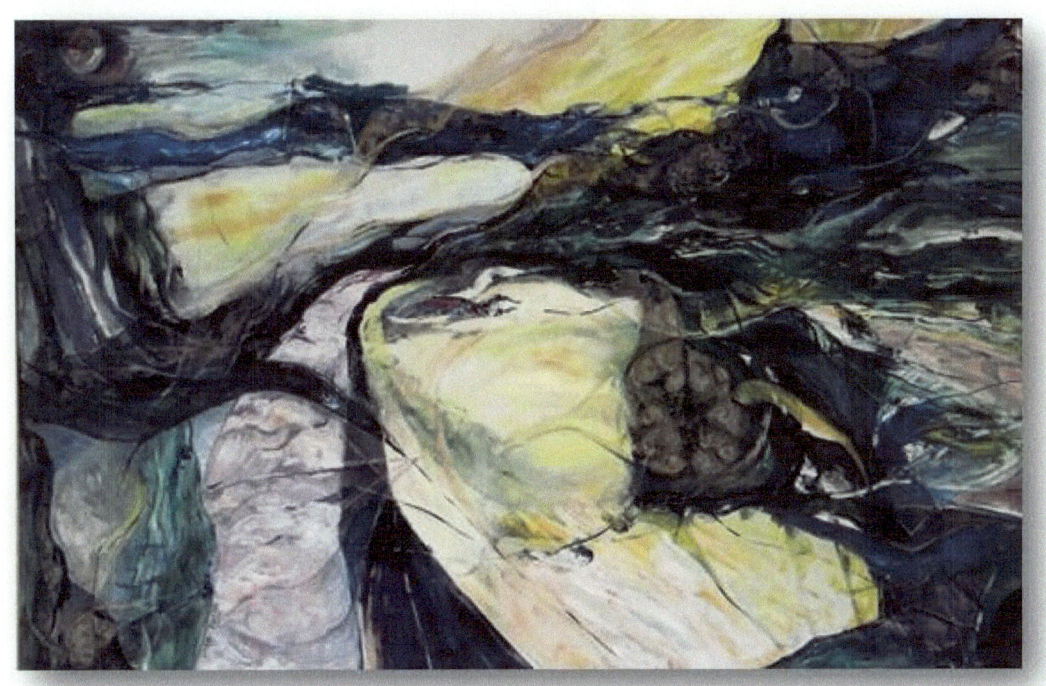

Acrylic on canvas, 80 by 120 cm

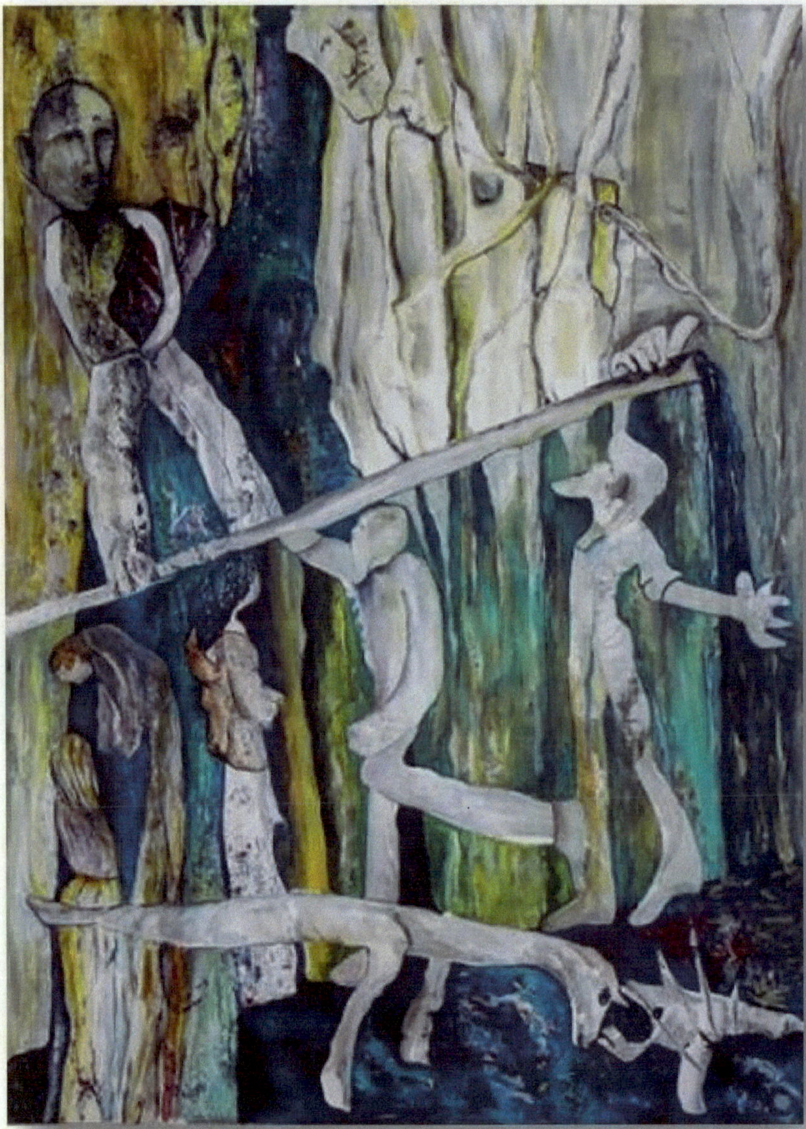

Acrylic on canvas, 122 by 88 cm

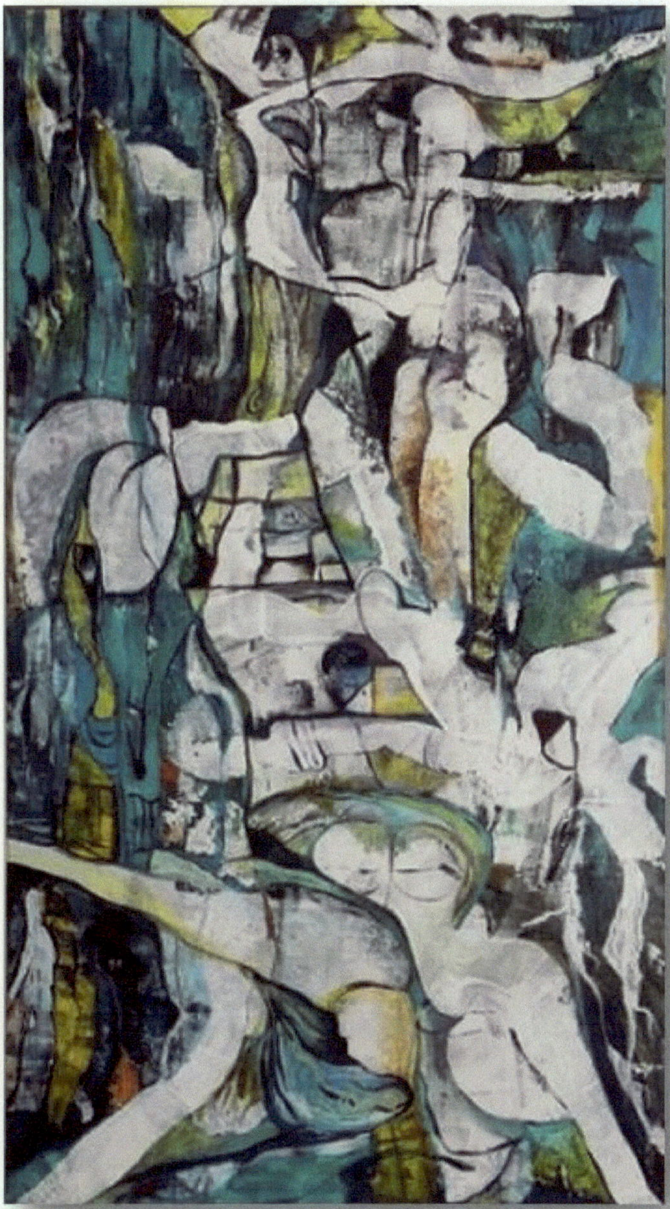

Acrylic on canvas, 113 by 64 cm

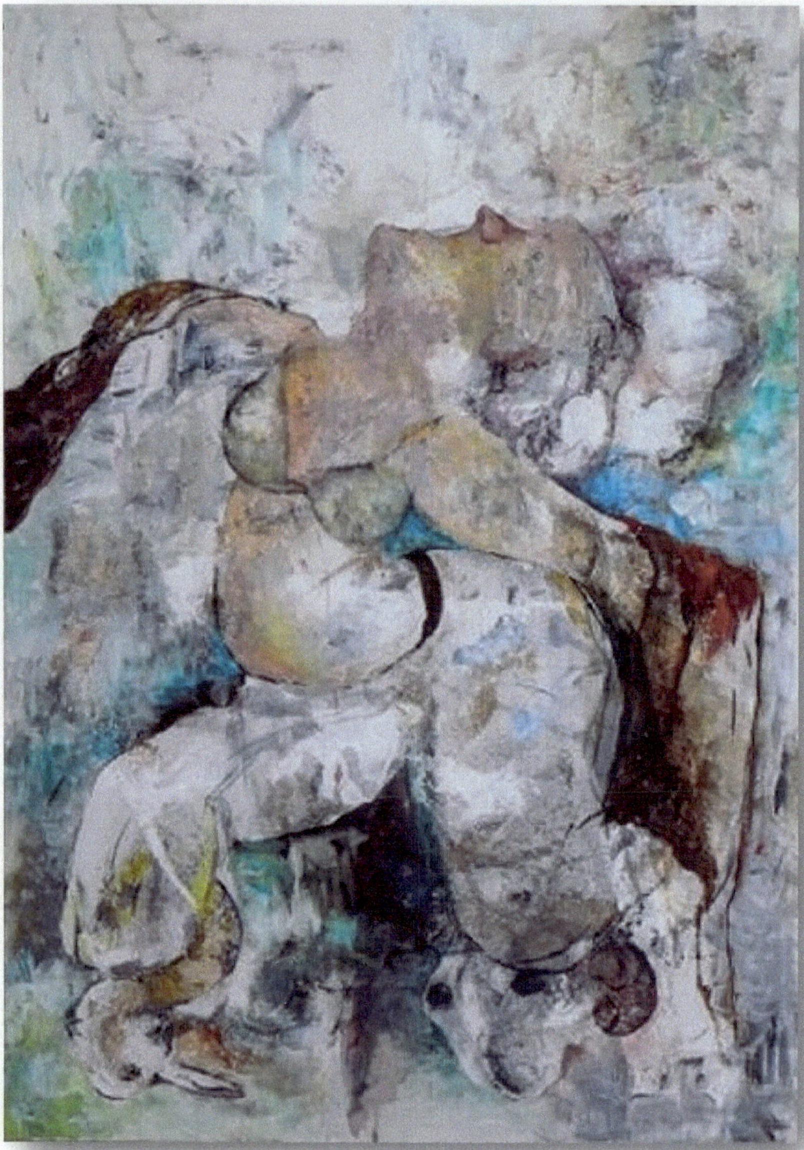

Acrylic on canvas, 100 by 70 cm

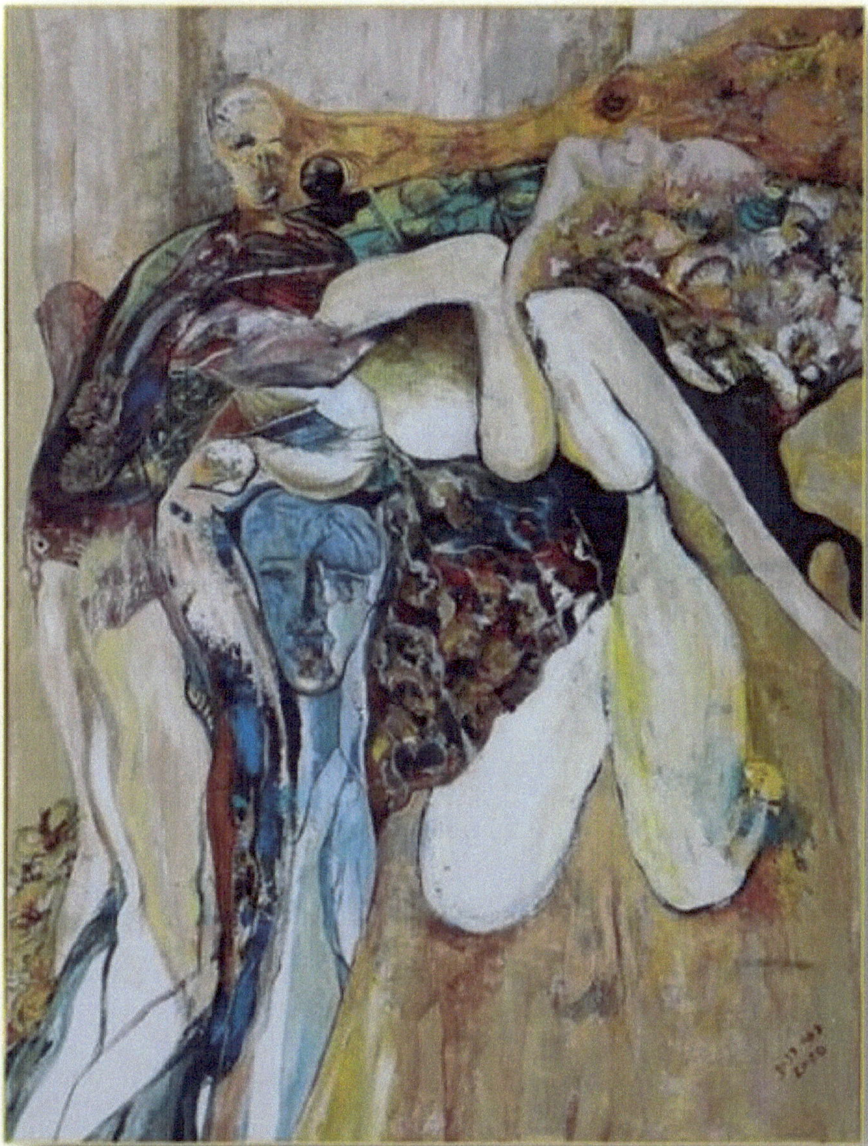

Acrylic on canvas, 80 by 60 cm

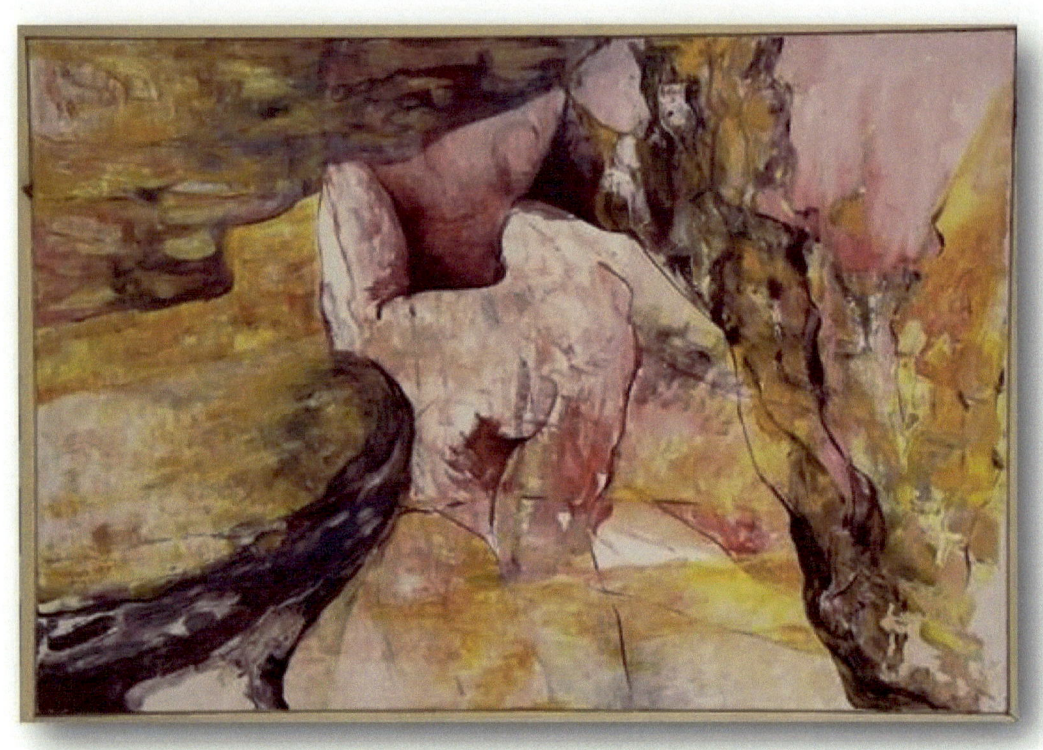

Acrylic on canvas, 70 by 100 cm

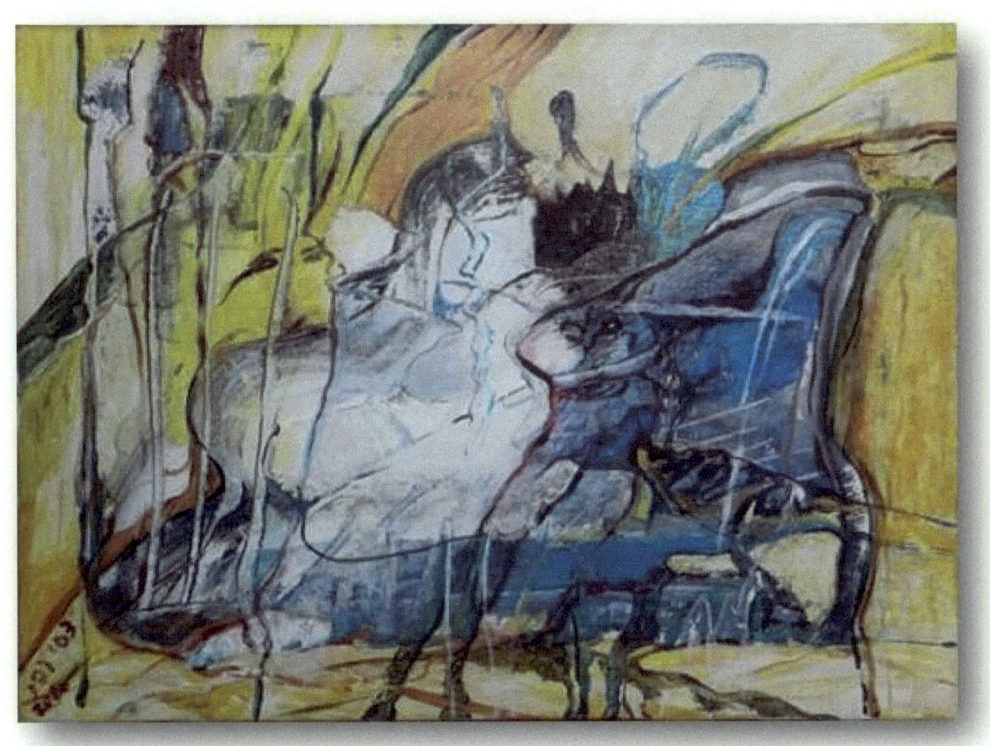

Acrylic on canvas, 30 by 40 cm

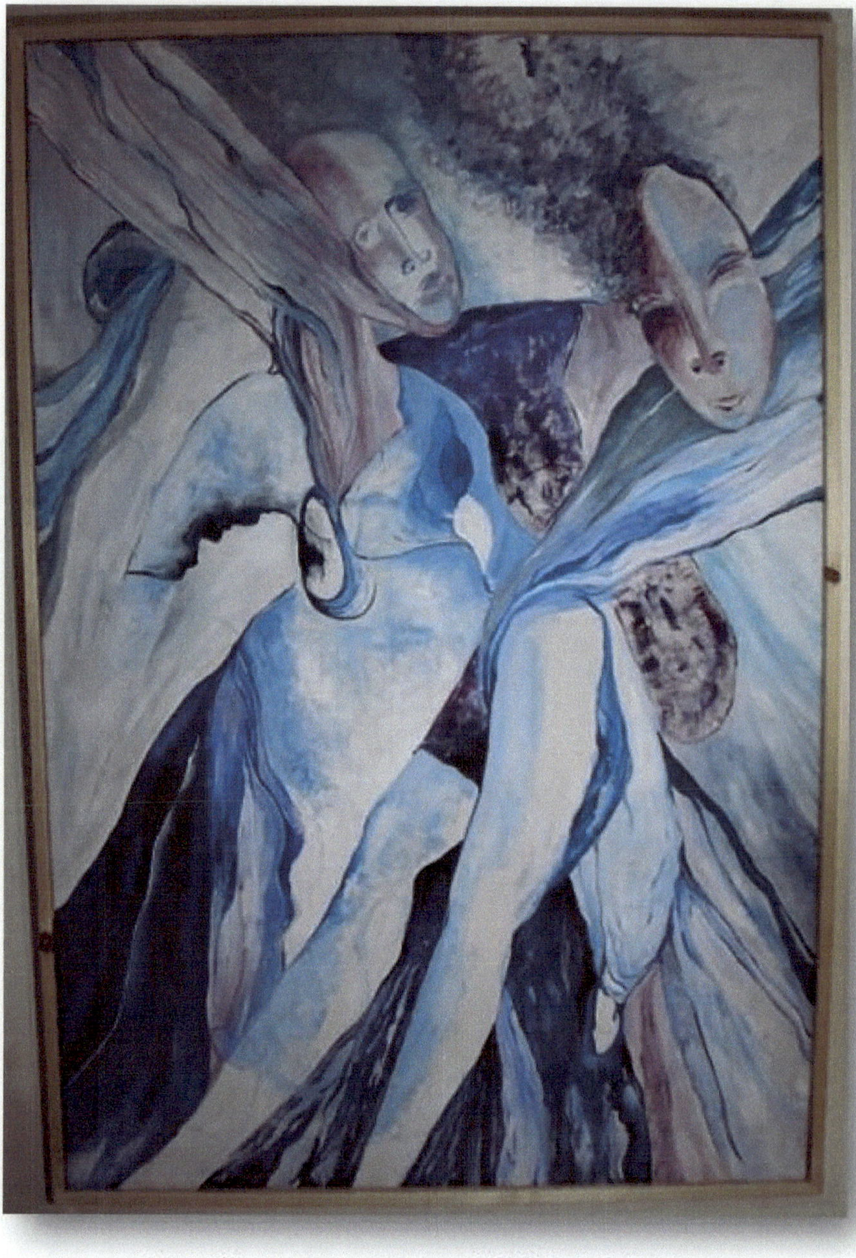

Acrylic on canvas, 120 by 80 cm

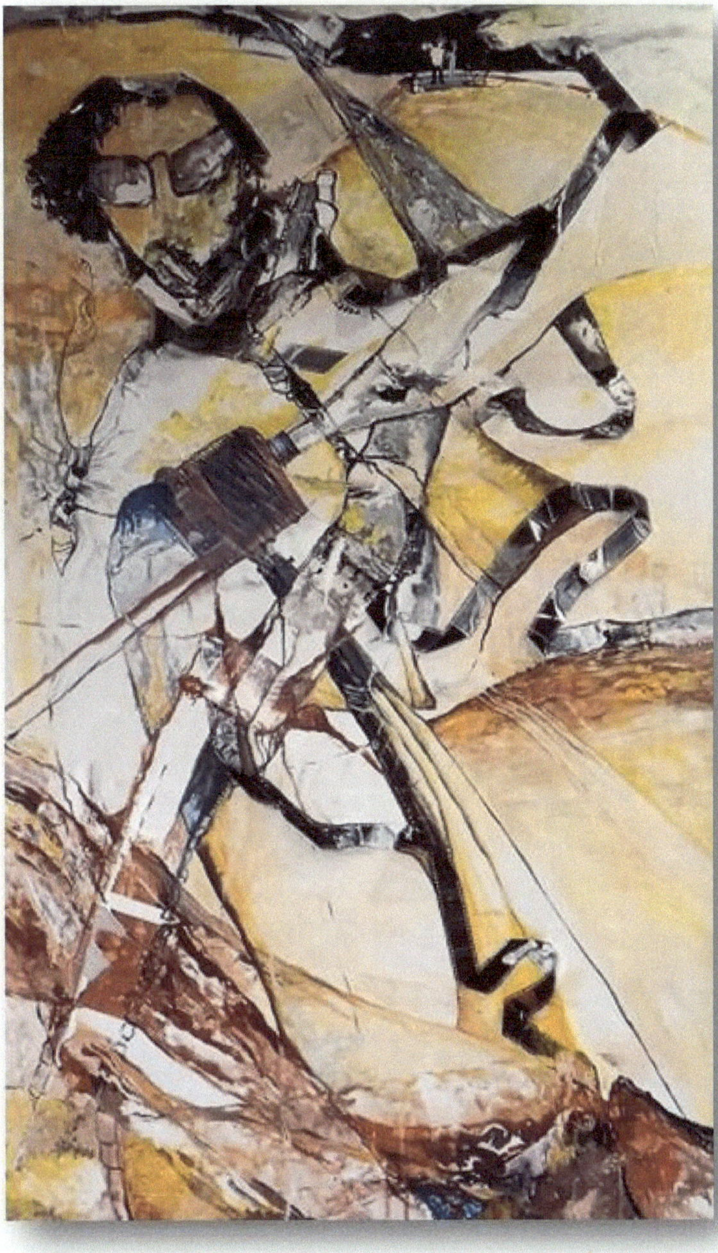

Acrylic on canvas, 170 by 105 cm

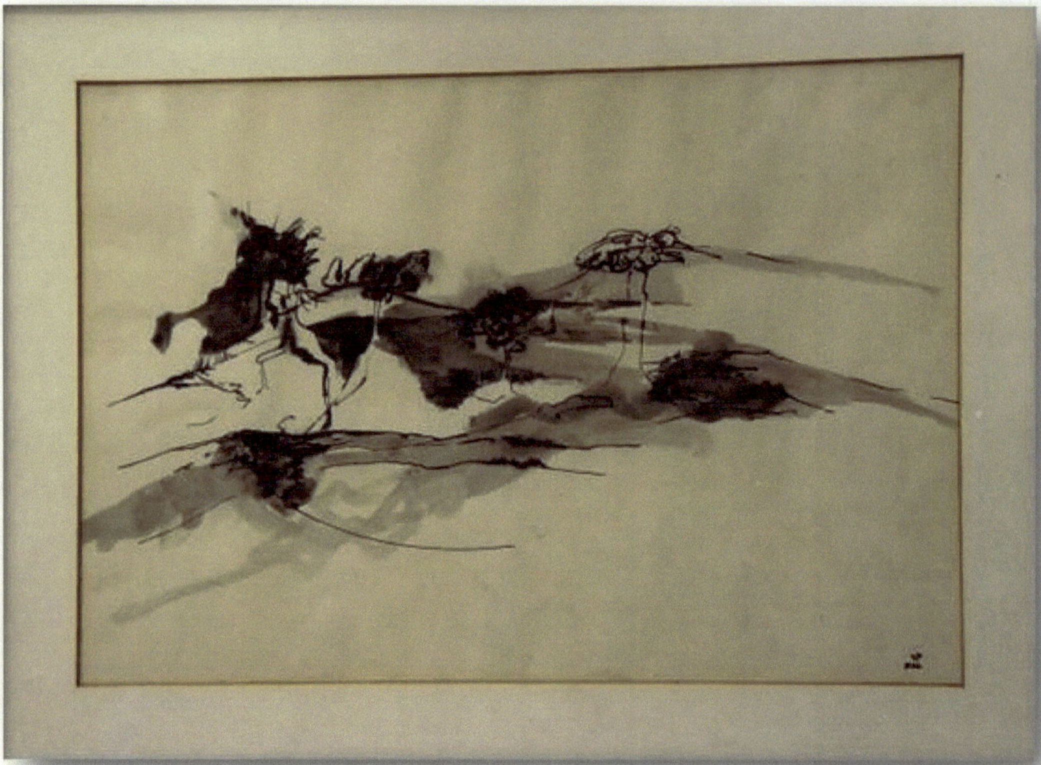

Watercolor on paper, 40 by 60 cm

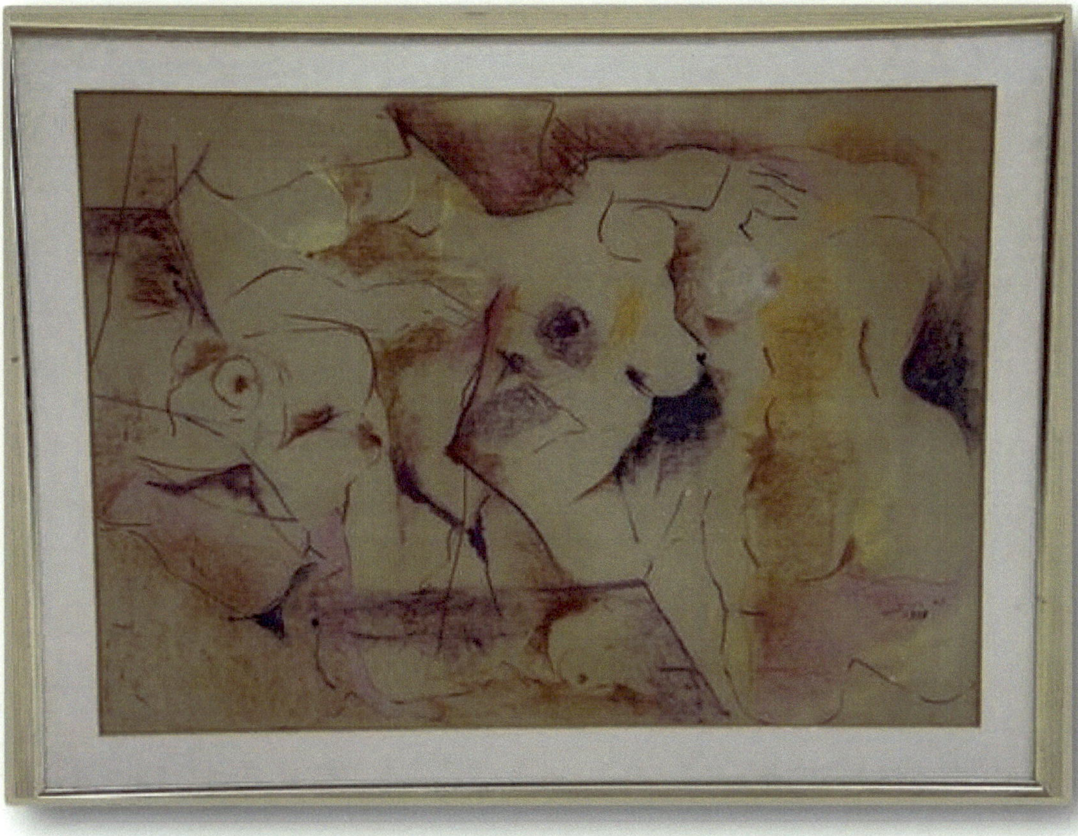

Pastel drawing on paper, 75 by 97 cm

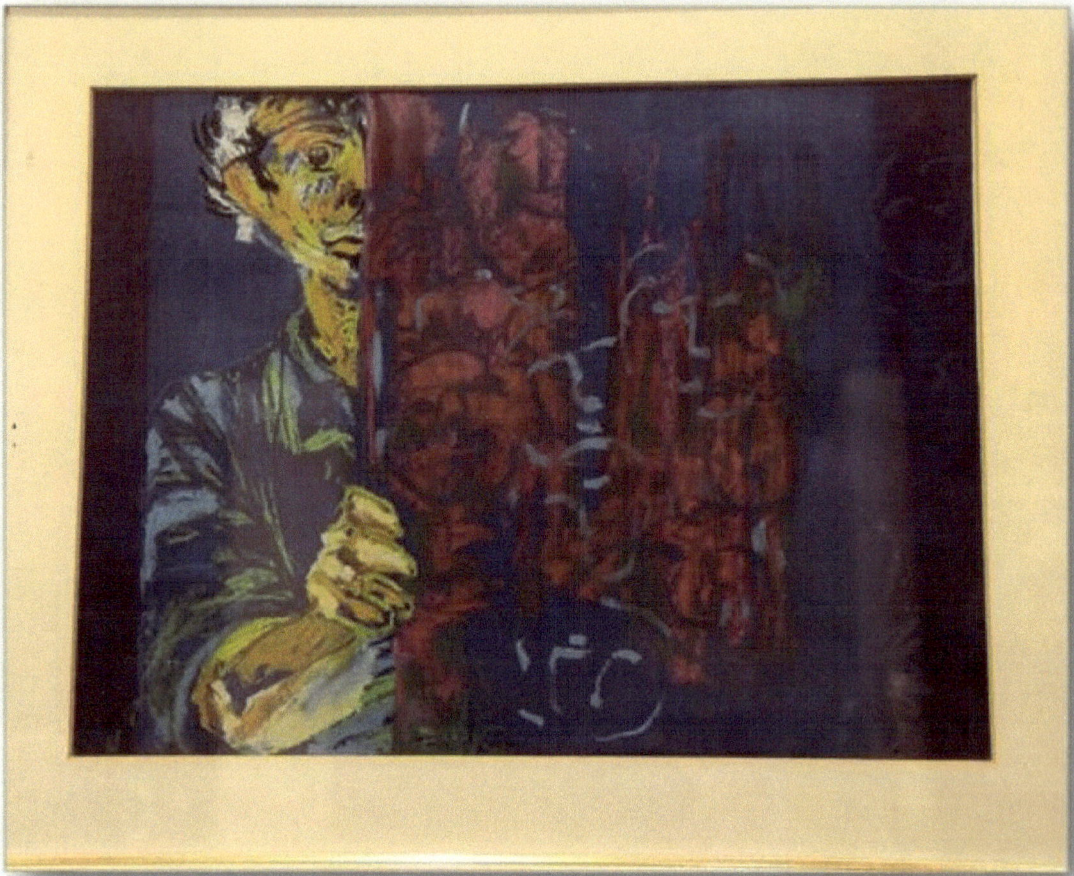

Pastel drawing on paper, 45 by 56 cm

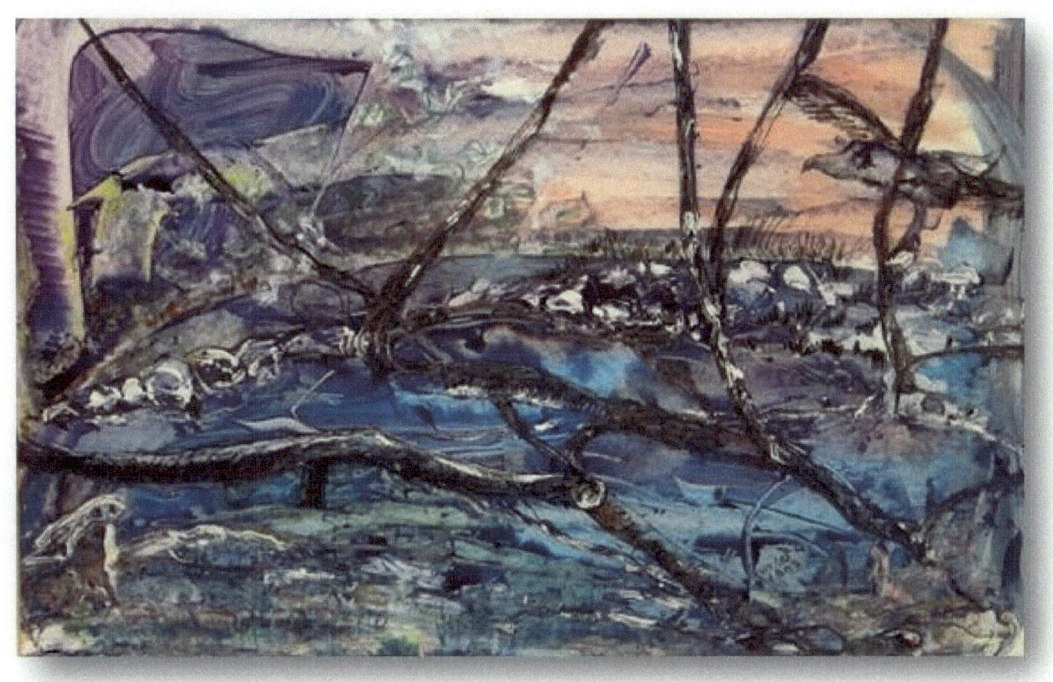

Acrylic and pastel on paper, 54 by 76 cm

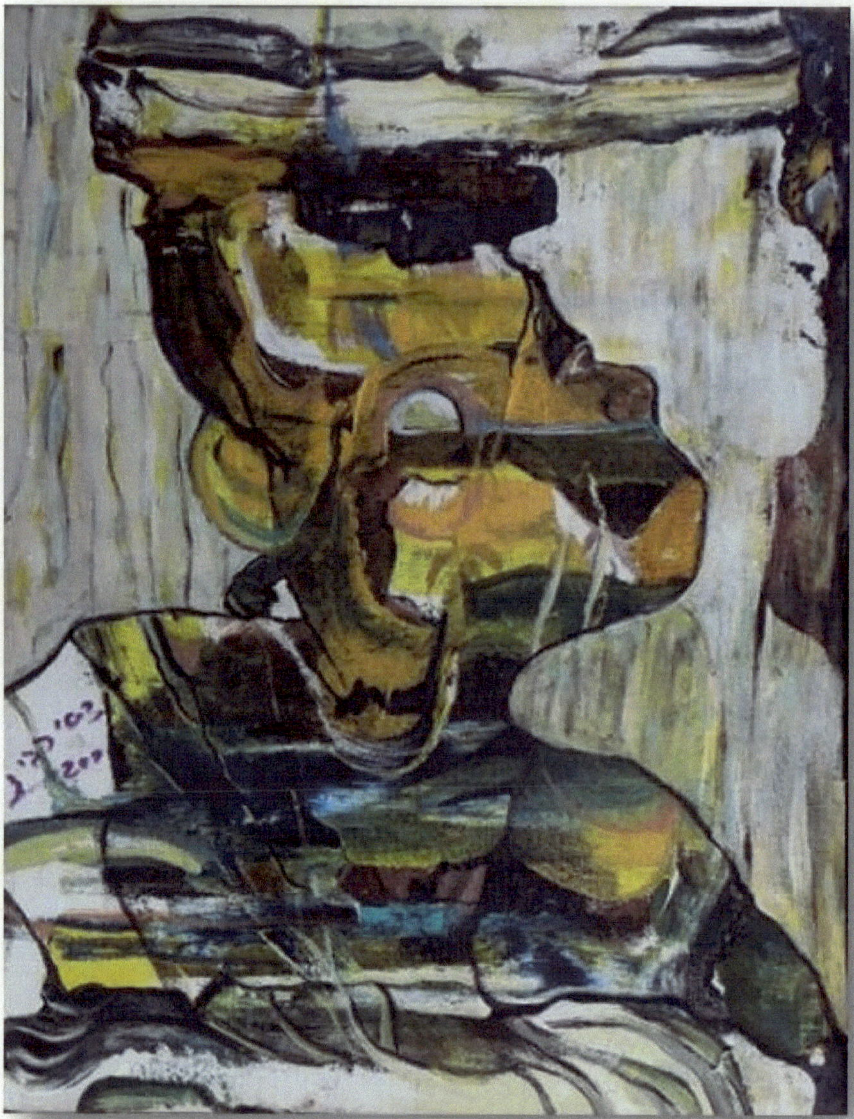

Acrylic on canvas, 33 by 26 cm

www.ingramcontent.com/pod-product-compliance
Lightning Source LLC
Chambersburg PA
CBHW040411220526
45473CB00004B/1200